# THAT WHICH WE ALREADY KNOW

By

Mark Robert Frank

Cover design and illustration by Sophie Binder of Sophie Binder Designs.

Author website: www.heartlandcontemplative.com

Print ISBN: 978-1-66784-845-7

This book is dedicated to Darla, my wife,
who stood by me and encouraged me
every step of the way.

# Table of Contents

# Preface

What does the world most need from us right now? If we were to ask this question of ten different people, we might get ten different responses. The world needs more love, more joy, more understanding. The world needs wisdom, awareness, and compassion. The world needs more gratitude, acceptance, generosity, and community. The world needs more peace. Who could argue with any of these? I certainly cannot. In my experience, though, the world needs something even more fundamental. The world needs more stillness.

The stillness that I'm referring to is likely not what most people think of when they hear the word. It's not the stillness of the desert or a deep forest glade. It's not the stillness to be found high up in the mountains above the tree line, where little moves but the wind. The stillness of which I speak is stillness of mind. Desert vistas, forest glades, and high mountain vantage points might be conducive to such stillness of mind, but they're not an absolute prerequisite. The mind can be still even in the most chaotic of situations, when all around is bustle and noise, or even violence.

But why is stillness of mind more fundamental to the world's well-being than love or any of those other attributes that are in such short supply? The answer is simple. Love, joy, understanding, wisdom, and awareness naturally arise out of stillness of mind. Compassion, gratitude, acceptance, and generosity all arise out of stillness of mind. Even community arises out of this stillness in the sense that the recognition of a deeply shared bond between all beings arises from it.

Unfortunately, stillness of mind is in short supply by the time we reach adulthood. Who has time for it amidst the bustle and noise of everyday life? And who can be convinced to make time for it with so many other "more pressing" concerns vying for attention? Such is the predicament of our maturity. Nevertheless, I do hope you're receptive to a gentle reminder. Stillness of mind is what this book is about.

Part childhood memoir, part spiritual enquiry, part psychological and philosophical exploration, what follows is an examination of one life nestled within the embrace of all life and all time and the stillness that exists at its core. We arise in this world with an innate capacity to experience stillness. There is nothing for us to learn in this regard. We simply need ease ourselves out of the way in order to realize how very much we already know.

# Introduction

The back gate of the very first home I ever knew opened onto a tract of land that I'll not forget for as long as I may live. Ostensibly, it served as the nursery for nearby Gerhardt Gardens. By the time I arrived on the scene, however, the various plots of shrubs and saplings had become so overgrown as to seem more like wilderness to the child that I was. If not exactly wilderness, it was a crazy quilt of different habitats stitched together and overlaid with whatever weeds, grasses, and woodland succession plants happened to have put down roots and begun working their way toward the sun. Notwithstanding its state of near abandonment, we still referred to those 20-odd acres of beautiful wildness as the Nursery. If nothing else, it was a nursery for young minds.

A well-worn path headed east from that gate, through a dark patch of woods squeezed between the corrugated steel fence of a contracting company and a thicket of white cedars within the

Nursery proper. It was there that my father hung for us a rope swing in a welcoming box elder tree still within view of our house. And it was just a little bit further along that path that a treehouse built by some older kids of days gone by beckoned to our new generation from high up in an imposing elm, challenging us to one day claim it as our own.

On the far side of that dark wood, the path opened onto the yard of an abandoned barn. Within its yawning embrace remained just enough rusting implements to be of interest to us kids, even as its formidable darkness, and the ricketiness of the steps leading up to its loft, kept our curiosity in check most of the time. We were much more likely to be found scampering after the multitude of skinks that made their home amongst the rocks and debris piled all along its most sunlit side.

The Gerhardts lived in a white stone mansion almost out of view of the front of that barn. We thought of it as a mansion, anyway, for we rarely saw one statelier. It had four white columns gracing its two-story face and stone chimneys either side. The Gerhardts, we'd been told, were the real owners of all that I've just begun to describe. Thus, we took care not to be seen as we passed by the back of their home. We didn't want any orders directed our way that we knew we could never obey.

A dirt road heading south from the mansion laid claim to the heart of the Nursery, an open space that once served as the staging area where harvested plants had their root wads wrapped in burlap prior to being carted up the hill to be sold. We only inferred this, though, from the remnants left behind. It was quite rare that we ever saw any of the workers. Only a couple of times each season would we see one puttering along on his tractor, flatbed cart in tow, sent there on a mission to abduct one of the tidier looking specimens. Nonetheless, these sightings always prompted a flurry of surveillance activity on our part. It was important that we ascertain the intentions of those intruders! To what part of our beloved realm had they been dispatched? And how much disruption would they cause?

A row of trees and blackberry brambles lined the far side of that road, beyond which a rolling meadow sloped from the outfield of a baseball diamond down to the nether reaches of our domain. The far side of that meadow was the eastern boundary of our world in those early years. Only on the rarest of occasions would we journey to its edge in order to oversee the activities of the men working in the stone yard next to the railroad tracks.

Another trail headed south from our back gate. It skirted the backyards of the homes on our side of the lane and provided access to the Nursery's interior via several footpaths branching off. Eventually it spilled onto a dirt road wending up the hill from that central staging area—past the bottom of our dead-end lane, the little vineyard up the way, and the old caretaker's farmhouse looking out onto the main thoroughfare.

It took a while for us to work up the courage to play amongst those vineyard rows. We'd make our way up the dirt road to where we could survey the premises from the safety of an adjacent cluster of bushes. Then, once satisfied our presence had gone undetected, we'd swoop in to scurry up and down the rows until a game of hide-and-seek invariably arose from our furtive exploration.

Gerhardt Gardens' retail space was just across that thoroughfare and down a little bit. We'd pass it on our drive to church on Sunday mornings, until the arrival of the interstate gave us a much more direct route there, that is. It overlooked the open field sloping down along the Nursery's southern boundary to that woodsy far corner below the ball field. Along the interior edge of that field were patches of prairie grass tall enough to get lost in, or tall enough to fashion into little hollows in which to while away an afternoon. The far edge bordered the back gardens of another neighborhood, the inhabitants of which we knew little about early on. That field was shared territory of a sort, navigated by us only warily in case the mysterious older boys were about.

The Nursery was graced with two great corridors of oaks. One was a veritable cathedral, with its entrance at the crossroads of several trails and a spacious interior that never failed to pull my gaze into its lofty canopy. It was a destination in its own right, or at least a place to visit for brief reflection while on the way to somewhere else. The other hall was a place of action and adventure. Its trees all had limbs so perfectly spaced as to tempt us to climb far higher than we were yet ready to climb.

Threading its way between that hall of climbing oaks and an airy stand of birch trees was a drainage ditch that carried stormwater from up above our lane down to a broad sinkhole about a hundred meters behind our neighbors' yard. We'd been warned to stay away from it, lest we tumble into its darkness and never again see the light of day. But that didn't stop us from throwing rocks into its gaping mouth in order to ascertain at least a little bit about its interior from the sounds that echoed back. And down the hillside from that sinkhole, just beyond where its discharge carved deep into a patch of sunchokes and Queen Anne's lace, was a grove of honey locust trees. Its thorny branches always gave us pause, as did the industrial detritus to be discovered there half-hidden in the grass and weeds.

Which brings me yet again to the low-lying corner of our realm—a vine-draped cluster of trees holding solemn vigil around a shallow basin into which the runoff from the entire watershed briefly gathered before disappearing under the railroad tracks for parts unknown. Our entire world flowed through that point: the winter showers dripping down lifeless stalks of prairie grass, the summer cloudbursts pummeling the wildflowers in the meadow rolling down from the ball field, the trickling mist from irrigation pipes watering the truck farmer's field further down the tracks, the rivulets gathering in the streets and sidewalks of civilization to gush into the darkness of the sinkhole and out again into the light. I must have sensed this even without the understanding that I presently have, for I was drawn there just as surely as the waters were. I'd meditate there while sitting on a fallen tree, without yet knowing that what I was doing had a name. I let my gaze soften, so as to take in everything and nothing all at once. The varied hues of green, the dancing flashes of sunlight piercing through the leafy curtains, the subtle impressions of form and light and being—I'd let them all flow through me like the water through that basin.

There was no shortage of sacred places in the Nursery that I knew. There was that patch of cool grass between the spruce and fruit trees where we lay with the scent of wild onions wafting up our nostrils. There were clusters of evergreen bushes forming cavern-like spaces underneath just big enough for us to crawl into and hide. There was a ring of mimosa trees with the trimmings of umpteen years piled high around its perimeter, just as the villagers did in my African adventure book in order to keep the lions at bay.

Yes, and there was that notch way up in the lone sycamore tree, the one that required no effort at all to rest in once you'd made it up that high. From there one could oversee the entire world that I've described thus far. There was the bottom of the ravine formed by the water washing down from the ball field. Everything seemed to disappear when we were there, save for the earth and sky. And there were all those little ponds wherever a bush or sapling had been plucked from the earth, leaving a hole in its place to gradually fill with rainwater. If you sat still beside one of them long enough, the frogs would begin to croak again, the birds would return to their chirping and singing, and a dragonfly might even light upon your knee. How still could I be? How long could I remain as one amidst so much sacred activity? I had no word for it then, but *suchness*[1] is the word that I would use for it now.

I learned a lot back there in the Nursery: the life cycles of frogs and mosquitoes, the coincidence of box elder trees and box elder bugs, the call of the crow, the red-winged blackbird, and the mourning dove, the look and feel and scent of various plants, and the earth in which they grew. I learned where you're likely to find a puffball and what will happen if you pop it when the time is right. I learned that that which is moist nurtures life and that which is dry welcomes rain. I learned that all of life is a transformation from one thing into another, a coming into being based on causes and conditions and a passing away once those causes and conditions pass away. I learned that nothing exists of its own accord and that stillness resides amid all this coming into being and passing away again.

Stillness was easy enough to find in the depths of winter, when everything was either dead or frozen. But it was there as well in a lonely birdcall on a sweltering afternoon. It was there in the blur

---

[1] *Suchness* refers to the sublime and ineffable nature of reality as experienced with unadorned awareness. *Suchness* and *thusness* are common translations of the Sanskrit word *tathata*.

of a dragonfly's wings—hovering and darting, hovering and darting. And it was there in the chorus of frogs that fell silent the moment our presence became known. What I appreciate most about the Nursery, however, from my position as one who is now "all grown up," was its ability to nurture in me that which I already knew: the value of sitting quietly, being watchful, and finding stillness deep within.

# Chapter 1: Eden

The Nursery was my Eden. For years I dwelt there in a state of childhood grace, wanting for nothing that wasn't already within reach. But just as the first humans were cast out of that mythical garden in a fall from grace that we ponder to this day, so I ponder my departure from that paradise and my fall from a state of being that only children and the very wisest among us can know.

"You may freely eat of every tree of the garden," that mythical first woman and man were told, "but you shall not eat of the tree of the knowledge of good and evil; for in the day that you eat of it, you will surely die."[2] As the story goes, Eve and Adam did eat of the forbidden fruit. But their death was not a physical one. What they died to was the state of grace they had previously enjoyed in their garden paradise.

---

[2] Genesis 2:16–17, World English Bible (WEB).

This story may be considered an allegory for what we now understand in more scientific terms. Our forebears rose from amongst all other species to possess the knowledge and self-awareness of *Homo sapiens*. Such intellect puts godlike power in our hands relative to the rest of the animal kingdom. It also comes with the incredible responsibility to use this knowledge wisely, lest we sow the seeds of our very own destruction.

Each of us falls from grace at some point on our long journey toward adulthood. We begin life in our own personal Eden of intimate union with all things. However, as the process of our individuation proceeds and our awareness of self and other becomes more refined, so begins our inexorable fall. The process of our coming of age invariably involves our eating fruit from the tree of the knowledge of good and evil, and in so doing we begin our fall from grace.

It might come tragically early, or it might come blessedly late. It might be precipitated by some traumatic event never to be forgotten, or it might occur so gradually as to leave not even a single remembrance of childhood's departure in its wake. Regardless, at some point we all gaze back through the mist of time to wonder of the child that we once were. What did we know then that we've forgotten along the way? Can we even begin to comprehend our loss?

Autumn was gloriously long the year I first began to fall, with crisp mornings and warm afternoons. Indian summer is what we called such weather, harking back in some barely understood way to a time when the gradual or abrupt onset of winter determined what life would be like in the coming months and years. Was there still time to augment the winter food stores, or must haste be made in order to ensure survival during the coming months of deprivation?

I was wondering then what life would be like in the coming months and years. Gone were the days when I could wake up of my own accord to then spend my hours in the Nursery as weather, whim, and the availability of companionship might dictate. Life had begun to make demands, and school had begun to seem like but a precursor to a dangerous new season of life. I'd seen things on the evening news and heard about them from the older kids. An endless summer of jungle warfare followed the spring of youth for so many young men, whether they were willing participants or not. The grown-up world was a troubled and troubling one, and my days were marching toward it.

Sweet respite from these concerns was what I sought as I closed the gate behind me and headed up the path between the thicket of white cedars and the airy stand of birch trees. Had it been the height of summer, I might have lingered in the soft undergrowth of Mayapples and wild ginger flourishing there in the relative coolness. On this day, however, it was light rather than shadow calling to me. It pulled my gaze beyond the drainage ditch and through the branches of the adjacent hall of climbing oaks to where the sunlight set aglow the clearing on the other side. It was sunlight that I needed, and solitude. And I knew precisely where to find them both.

Just past the birch grove, the trail skirted the sinkhole and angled across a grassy clearing. The sounds of home were far behind me now, replaced by the lingering croaking of frogs coming from the many ponds on the clearing's far side. I continued across the dirt road heading south from Gerhardt mansion, then down into a shallow swale and up the other side until I'd reached the heart of the meadow rolling down from the baseball diamond.

The ravine was invisible to anyone approaching from the west—hidden, as it was, by the tangle of wasting wildflowers spilling over its edge. That and the fact that there were only businesses off to the east made it unlikely that I'd have any intruders from that direction for as long as I chose to stay there. I scrambled down the earthen wall and settled into a cupped space along the opposite bank. The bare earth felt both soft and solid against my back. It cushioned, supported, and surrounded me, even as the sky above remained as deep and open as ever. The sun felt warm on my body, and the air was still. It was quiet, too, given that the stirrings of the remaining insects up above in the meadow were directed skyward. Only occasionally was the sound of a red-winged blackbird loud enough to make its presence known. Its sharpness pierced the air before trailing off into silence.

I studied the earthen bank and dug my fingers into the moist coolness below the surface. I studied the occasional crawling being that let itself be known. I studied the sky—milky blue and almost clear, save for a scant few wispy clouds that seemed to barely move. And when my eyes grew tired of studying what was going on around me, I took to studying the way the sun shone through the red flesh of my eyelids. No, nothing much was going on at the bottom of that ravine, but that was good. Far too much was going on back in the world I'd left behind. That world wanted something from me, and I wasn't quite sure what. This one wanted nothing from me but my ability to observe.

The passage of time becomes difficult to track when there's not much going on. Our experience of it becomes more subjective. Perhaps our mind begins to wander, becoming disassociated from any cues in the outside world. Perhaps our thinking slows to the point that its pace ceases to be a reliable measure. The calling bird, chirping cricket, and wriggling earthworm all mark time in their respective ways. In the absence of anything else, our very own breath creates our "minutes." Our beating heart ticks off our "seconds." Time ceases to be something that we move through— if, in fact, it ever was. It becomes something that we are.

I came to notice a bulbous formation about the size of a quarter midway up one of the dried goldenrod stalks angling over the edge of the ravine. Curious, I climbed up, snapped it from its stem, and returned to my place. It was woody but light. I tapped it against a flat rock that happened to be sitting there beside me. Maybe it was hollow. Maybe it wasn't. I rolled it around in my fingers and scratched it with my fingernail. What was it? And why had such a thing formed in the first place?

Notwithstanding this mystery, or perhaps because of it, I took to being time by filing off the little nubs where the stem had entered and exited the bulb. I rubbed them against the rock until what remained was like a solid wooden bead. I then sat with it in the palm of my hand, watching the almost imperceptible movement of the clouds and watching my own being marking time from moment to moment.

I spent the afternoon that way. At times I merely watched. Occasionally I crafted another bead from one of the odd stems that I'd come to realize were more abundant than I'd thought. I had four of them in my pocket by the time I finally climbed out of the ravine for the return walk home. It was growing cool, and I was growing hungry. My mother would surely be preparing dinner. After dinner, we'd watch some television or maybe I'd work on one of my model cars. No, the circumstances that had prompted me to go off to be alone weren't any different, but at least I was able to return with just a little bit of the stillness that I'd been reminded of out there in the ravine.

I don't recall what became of those beads that I and nature crafted all those years ago. I kept them in a little bowl on my bookshelf for a time, but then I lost track of them. It's funny then that I still remember them after all this time. Perhaps they represent for me the great mystery that we carry around with us day in and day out—the mystery of our very existence. We usually keep it tucked away in our most secret pocket, only occasionally pulling it out to ponder for a moment before tucking it away again. Maybe we believe that we've left such questions far behind. But that's never really the case. The mystery remains quite unresolved, hovering on the periphery of consciousness for the remainder of our lives.

Greater mysteries notwithstanding, I did finally learn why those bulbous growths form on some goldenrod stems. They're created when a goldenrod fly lays its eggs inside the stem. Once the eggs hatch and the larvae begin feeding, the plant responds by creating a woody formation around them, a gall. If the larvae are fortunate, they'll make their way out of the gall as fully grown flies the following spring. If not, they'll become a meal for a foraging woodpecker or chickadee. Curiously, though, even the luckiest goldenrod fly enjoys but a fleeting existence. Fully mature adults don't even eat!

Relative to the goldenrod fly, my own existence has been a long one, long enough for me to consider my own and our collective fall from grace. Is it possible to know our Eden once again as children do, without the separation that accompanies our heightened sense of self-awareness? This question was on my mind as I walked in the park the other day, one quite beautiful and natural in appearance despite being surrounded by a sprawling cityscape.

I stood for a time on a bridge there gazing down at some turtles sunning themselves amidst the flotsam backed up alongside the bridge abutment. I was struck by how unperturbed they were by the plastic bottles and sundry other garbage floating in their midst. It occurred to me that I was witnessing something of what I'd lost long ago in my fall from childhood grace.

Upon reflection, the Nursery was not the most pristine of natural environments either. I suppose you could call it a managed resource. To us children, though, it was wilderness. Neither was the stream separating the birch grove from the hall of climbing oaks a naturally flowing one. It was more an extension of the storm drains up the way, silted in with whatever had been scoured from the roofing shingles and asphalt pavement in and beyond our little neighborhood. To us, though, it was a treasure. Similarly, those industrial castoffs half-hidden in the grass beneath the honey locust trees were curiosities worthy of exploration much more than they were eyesores. And while that deep gash of a ravine carved into the meadow sloping down from the ball field would no doubt have me lamenting the maltreatment of the land if I were to see it for the first time today, back then I saw nothing of the sort. It was a rugged canyon, a lunar landscape, a meeting place, and a refuge.

The Nursery was my beloved realm, notwithstanding the blemishes and imperfections my adult mind imposes on my memories of it. Likewise, that urban waterway is the beloved realm of turtles, fish, and waterfowl, regardless of the trash washed there that gives me pause. For just as animal discernment is oriented toward that which promotes life, so a child's discernment is oriented toward that which induces wonder. Discrimination and judgment will come later, after our having eaten from the tree of the knowledge of good and evil.

Undoubtedly those turtles were no less content amidst the flotsam of that city park than if they'd been sunning themselves on their favorite old-growth cypress log in the depths of a sleepy backwater. Nature is like that. It doesn't proceed in full or half measure depending upon circumstance. It always proceeds in full measure. The windblown seed likewise has no knowledge of whether it will put down roots, or where. But if conditions are right, it will sprout and reach toward the sun with all the energy it can muster. Whether in a garbage-strewn alleyway or a beautiful country meadow, it greets each moment with everything it is. Children are like that too, living fully and completely without regard for circumstance.

Do you recall such days lived without any sense of separation, with trust and acceptance, with mind and body seamlessly integrated one with the other and together with all things? Do you recall being unconstrained by worry, judgment, conceptualization, and doubt? This is the freedom of children and the wisest among us, and everything else that resides in the natural world—the freedom to be precisely what we are and nothing we are not—the freedom to live completely, fearlessly, and spontaneously.

Children don't simply know this freedom; they embody it. Ironically, our developing self-awareness brings this freedom into view just as it begins to disappear, like sunlight creating a rainbow in the mist even as it boils that mist away. My heart was heavy with this awareness as I embarked on that solemn walk, past the birch grove and across the dirt road heading down from Gerhardt mansion, to spend the afternoon sitting in the ravine in the middle of the meadow rolling down from the baseball diamond. Yes, the sound of frogs emanating from the many ponds that I knew so well still sang inside my heart. Yes, I still felt deeply my connection to that patch of earth and all that lived upon it. But darkness lurked just over the horizon. A war was being fought somewhere out there in the grown-up world. And one day, I would be a grown-up too.

The passing years of my then short life had placed the fruit of the tree of the knowledge of good and evil upon my tongue, and without even realizing what was happening I'd begun to chew and swallow. Call it the natural development of human intellect and self-awareness. Call it original sin. Regardless, my fall from grace was underway and gathering speed. For what is a first grader to do except contemplate the second and then the third grade after that? And because I could, I counted them off until the twelfth. But what came after that, beyond where the school years reached? What came after was a dangerous future that I could scarcely comprehend.

The specter out there on the horizon was becoming more real with each dark glimpse, cleaving my mind from my body, leaving me a stranger where I was. Image upon image, the future took shape: television footage of soldiers dropping from helicopters into rice paddies and muddy jungle clearings, a classmate speaking of his older brother's draft number being drawn, a photograph in a magazine of a gun being held to the temple of a frightened little man and the trigger being pulled.

Ah, but grace was still so close at hand, and closer still within the embrace of my beloved realm! In the Nursery, there was only the present moment. In the Nursery, the seamless nature of body and mind returned. There, I was freedom once again. There, I was oneness—like in the summer before that autumn, with my fully functioning childhood blossoming in all its glory.

I can still feel what it was like to ride my bike along the winding dirt roads and trails, engaging every dip, rise, and root. We would explore from after breakfast on, returning only when our hunger called us or to kneel for gulps of water from the shaded backyard spigot. I can still taste that metallic water and smell my mother's mint flourishing there in the moist earth beneath the dripping faucet. And I remember heading off again, with the warm sun on my face and cool water down the front of my T-shirt.

There was only that which was. And in the complete acceptance of that which was there was sufficiency, contentment, and peace. Nothing required improvement. Nothing needed to change. There was neither enlightenment nor attainment, neither journey nor spirituality. There was only being. Being has no need for words or concepts. Being actualizes itself regardless of how we might try to describe it. Perhaps we adults read these words and call them knowledge, but a child has no need for them at all! Children already embody every bit of wisdom that they need.

# Chapter 2: Our Fall

Where did that Eden go? Where did that child go? My fall from grace happened so quickly that within just a few short years hardly a trace of either remained. Thankfully, I didn't have to go off and fight in that distant war. It ended years before my number might have been drawn. But by then my Eden was gone, and the child who once lived there was nowhere to be found. I could blame it on the war. I could say that I was just another of its many uncounted casualties—the ones who never lost a drop of blood. The fact is, though, I would have fallen anyway. We all end up falling sooner or later. It's simply part of being human. What exactly does that mean though? In order to answer that question, we'll need to reflect more deeply on what really happened back there in that mythical garden.

Legend has it that Adam and Eve were created by God and given dominion over all living things. Despite having the intellect necessary for such mastery, however, they were also both naked and without shame. On one hand, we might interpret this as Adam and Eve still being like all the other animals, or like children perhaps, without any notions regarding the "wrongness" of being unclothed. On the other hand, we might think of this nakedness in metaphorical terms. They'd not yet become clothed with any ideas of separate selfhood. It wasn't just that they were unaware that they'd done something wrong. They were unaware of being separate beings in the first place. They had enough knowledge to dwell in mastery over all the other creatures of the natural world, but they'd not yet set themselves apart from it.

The authors of the Genesis story were striving to understand their place in the world, just as we modern humans are. We're just more likely to lean on the theory of evolution instead of legend when we do. We take it for granted, now that we have it, but self-awareness didn't always exist. It takes a brain of certain complexity, which our human ancestors didn't always possess. Nonetheless, somewhere deep in the shadows of prehistory, the *one who knows* became the *one who knows that he knows*, and it was then that the most resourceful of animals became something altogether different. Suddenly, relative to the vast expanse of time since the inception of life on earth, one being stood apart from all others. Rising like a third dimension out of the flatness of the more ordinary consciousness that humans share with other animals, self-awareness gave our forebears unprecedented consciousness relative to that of all other beings.

It's worth noting that the only warning Adam and Eve were given regarding the fruit of the tree of the knowledge of good and evil was that eating it would cause them to die. It was the serpent, without actually possessing any godlike knowledge of its own, that suggested that the fruit could open their eyes and give them knowledge of good and evil. What Adam and Eve really obtained, though, was self-awareness, and with that newfound self-awareness arose a sense of nakedness. What they died to was the natural belongingness that they'd previously enjoyed without question. They were henceforth separated from the natural order, their natural instincts having been supplanted by human concepts of sufficiency and lack, contentment and inadequacy, and, yes, right and wrong.

But what exactly made something right or wrong in that prehistoric world not yet touched by law or religion? Was the right thing to do merely a learned behavior that was reinforced by the fact that it enhanced the likelihood of survival, or was the right thing to do based on that newly emergent self-awareness leading to the recognition of the intrinsic worth of others as well? Perhaps there was an interplay between the two.

Evidence exists that we humans and our forebears have been burying our dead and caring for our sick and elderly for a hundred thousand years or more. It makes sense that the emergence of self-awareness must have given rise to at least some rudimentary sense of right and wrong with respect to caring for each other in sickness, old age, and death. Patterns of behavior that evolved and persisted over millennia due to their tendency to enhance group survival must have come to be seen as right once the intellectual capacity to reflect upon them finally evolved.

The sick might get well and return to helping the group with its hunting, gathering, and other survival-oriented tasks. Expending time and resources nursing them back to health must have been seen as a good investment. Similarly, the aged, notwithstanding their waning physical abilities, would still have possessed a wealth of valuable knowledge related to animal behavior and the location and use of medicinal plants. Even funerary rites might have served a utilitarian purpose. They likely helped foster the social cohesion necessary for survival in a dangerous world. Showing respect for the deceased would have allowed each individual to affirm to others that he or she was a committed member of the group. In turn, this would have helped foster commitment of the group to that individual. Thus, behavior that we modern humans think of as right and civilized could have come into existence via a process of natural selection long before the emergence of the self-awareness possessed today.

But natural selection only goes so far toward explaining the development of the ideas of right and wrong that occurred between those days when Neanderthals first began burying their dead and the unprecedented blossoming of religious and moral enquiry characteristic of the Axial Age.[3] Whereas the former might be explained as reinforced behavior evident within groups of interdependent individuals, the latter encompasses recognition of the intrinsic worth of even one's mortal enemies, something that is difficult to explain in terms of natural selection alone.

A perfect example of an Axial Age religious text that grapples with self-awareness and ideas of right and wrong is the Bhagavad Gita. The Gita tells of one despairing warrior, Arjuna, surveying the battlefield on which his clan and another, each with warriors that he both loves and respects, would fight to the death on the following day. Arjuna's charioteer, who is actually his Lord Krishna disguised to mortal eyes, then speaks to him consolingly and encouragingly of the various paths to liberation that are available to him.

The existence of such a text is difficult to explain in strictly utilitarian terms. On the contrary, altruistic ideas regarding our shared humanity are all too clearly present in Arjuna's despair— ideas that can't be explained away except by interpreting the Gita as a callous exhortation that Arjuna dispense with his existential dithering and fight for the sake of his progeny. No, by then knowledge of good and evil had grown far too intrusive. Self-

---

[3] A period of parallel religious development that occurred in the first millennium BCE.

awareness had grown far too acute for the quandary of Arjuna and others like him to be dismissed so easily. A pack of hyenas does not ponder the rightness or wrongness of its survival instincts. Such torments are the plight of humankind alone.

We also know that this emerging concern for other beings did not manifest as concern for human beings alone. Early Native Americans, for instance, considered themselves part of a natural order that they could behave in accord with or not. The natural order was one in which an elk or a bear allowed itself to be taken as long as the hunters proved worthy. If the hunter failed to act with respect toward and a sense of shared bond with his prey, the hunt would be in jeopardy. Where would such thinking come from if not the emergence of self-awareness and the resultant recognition of the intrinsic worth of other beings as well?

At this point, you may be wondering about the downside of the emergence of self-awareness. A newfound awareness that there is a right and a wrong way to treat our fellow tribe members and rivals alike would seem to be a good thing, wouldn't it? A newfound realization that we should bring sacred awareness to our relationship with other inhabitants of this earth would seem to be a positive development, wouldn't it? What is the downside of our banishment from Eden? Indeed, it might seem that self-awareness is without a dark side.

The difficulty is that, even as self-awareness has helped foster the spiritual recognition of the unity of all things, it has led to the ascendancy of the self as the most important of human concerns. These two conflicting potentialities—the ability to act on our recognition of the unity of all things and the ability to act in the most self-serving ways—are now central to the human condition. Compassion and concern for the common good pull us in one direction. Self-survival concerns pull us in the other. From the wandering bands of Neanderthals burying their few dead to the terrible destructive power of modern nation-states at war, from the hunter-gatherers striving to feed themselves in accord with the natural order to our factory farming practices that treat animals as non-sentient resources to be mined, from the first transcendent recognition of the oneness of all things to the so-called "rightness" of the barriers that we erect between self and other, so the nature of self-awareness, the knowledge of good and evil, and the fall of humankind have progressed.

Each of us recapitulates the achievement of human evolution over the course of normal human development. Each of us rises from our "flat" consciousness to look about and survey a world of self and other. The undifferentiated oneness of early infancy gives way to our first inkling of a world that is other than our very own body. From there we begin the inexorable march toward the fully individuated ego strength of adulthood. Neurological development becomes the ground for psychological development. Psychological development, in turn, precipitates further neurological development. Our body and mind continue to grow and adapt from day to day. In this way, our personal "fall from grace" mirrors that of all humankind. The child who knows becomes the child who knows that she knows. It is then that she begins to fall.

Once self-awareness has arisen, it becomes difficult to think of life as being about anything other than its experience. Whatever joys, sorrows, and reflections might follow on the heels of this milestone of development invariably become incorporated into our conceptualization of the so-called meaning of life. Rare is the adult who, upon contemplating the entirety of his or her existence, concludes that the meaning of life resides in something that he or she experienced way back in childhood—no matter how idyllic a childhood it might have been. Instead, we tend to think of this body as we do a flowering plant. Just as the roots, stems, and leaves of a rose bush seem to exist for the sole purpose of producing an exquisite blossom, so we think of self-aware consciousness as the raison d'etre of the human organism.

The development of self-awareness results in our identifying more and more with our thought processes and less and less with the organism that makes them possible. We begin to speak of our bodies and their constituent parts as we might speak of the house and the possessions of the homeowner living inside. In reality, though, while we might cut the rose blossom from the bush and place it in a vase of water for a time, the human mind is impossible to separate from its roots, stems, and leaves.

"Mind is what the brain does" is a phrase that's often used to describe the relationship between mind and brain. But the brain does not merely do what's inside of the cranium in which it is housed. The brain is connected by nerves and blood vessels to all other parts of the body—checking their orientation in space and sampling whatever biochemical information they might have to convey. It would seem then that the mind is not just what the brain does; the mind is what the body does. But why stop there? The brain, via the various sense organs that it innervates, monitors everything with which the body comes into contact. For instance, despite the ninety-three million miles between them, the sun and the eye still combine to create vision—an experience that sets the mind to reflecting upon light and wondering about its nature. Thus, it's not so outrageous to say that mind is the entire world, although such a statement might take some getting used to, given the way we normally think about things.

From the perspective of infancy, however, "mind is the entire world" makes perfect sense. In that oceanic state of undifferentiated oneness, the infant does not yet perceive any separation between self and other. There is not yet a conception of a self to which anything might exist in contrast. It is only with subsequent neurological development and further exploration of his or her surroundings that the infant begins to view the world in such a way. Fuzzy at first, perceived boundaries become crisper over time. Once-tentative conceptualizations related to our body, our mind, our life, the world, and our possessions begin to take on a sense of absolute solidity.

I've long been intrigued by the ability of young children to withstand all manner of hardship that a more mature individual would find thoroughly devastating. How is it that young children can respond with such resiliency to life-threatening disease and natural disaster, poverty and war, disfiguring accident and disabling trauma, or the loss of a parent? The answer, in large part, is that young children don't yet possess the strong sense of self that leads to such suffering. While the pain and difficulty of whatever harsh circumstances the child faces are still present, absent is anguish born of perceived inequity, the foreshortening of an imagined life, or the loss of faith or existential meaning. Such suffering is predicated on a strong sense of self. Therein lies the wisdom of children.

The blossom of childhood wisdom begins to unfold as the more passive state of oceanic oneness gives way to a relatively active state of independent exploration. At this time, the child possesses just enough self-awareness that he may explore the world without undue risk of harm but not so much as to precipitate separation from it. His "vision" has not yet become distorted with the belief, conceptualization, fear, and desire that inevitably accompany the creation of the self.

We don't usually think of wisdom being present at such a tender age. Rather, we think of it as something that only those long in years may come to possess. And we certainly don't think that we possess it at the time. But it is precisely the absence of any notion that she possesses anything at all that makes the blossoming wisdom of childhood all the more exquisite and profound. If only its bloom could be preserved into adulthood! What a different world we would enjoy! Ah, but all too soon the harsh glare of self-awareness will turn that blossom into little more than a desiccated memory pressed between the pages of our book, to be wondered about from time to time and spoken of nostalgically.

Some people speak as if the spirit of the child that they once were has taken leave, perhaps to dwell unchanged in an alternative universe far away. Others speak as if that child remains within us to this day, buried deep beneath our psychic rubble, patiently awaiting his recovery. But such ideas are merely figments of the adult imagination, projecting existing experiences of selfhood onto the past.

Life can be thought of more accurately as a fountaining forth from the ground of existence as conditions arise and a passing away as those conditions subside. When we gaze at a fountain rising out of a pool of water, we perceive solidity where there is merely an ongoing process of water flowing forth and returning again to the pool. Of course, we humans are so much more complex and long-lived in a relative sense, but in principle we are the same. From moment to moment and day to day, the cells of our body arise and pass away, then to be replaced by others in a dynamic process that maintains the appearance of static existence, despite reality being otherwise.

This fountaining forth continues throughout our lifetime, gradually changing over time such that the infant becomes the child, the child develops into the youth, and the youth matures into the adult—one transitioning into another so seamlessly as to be without any true demarcation. Throughout this process, consciousness continues with "eyes" that change ever so gradually over time. Just as our physical eyes become afflicted with cataracts and other obscurations that draw attention to themselves instead of the view that exists outside, so our vision of the world becomes distorted with belief, conceptualization, fear, and desire—thereby drawing attention to the created self.

Rather than being something intellectual, the wisdom of childhood is the fully integrated wisdom of body and mind, unencumbered by those aspects of developed selfhood that will eventually come to obscure or constrain it. I'll explore this wisdom further in a subsequent chapter. For now, though, let me close this one by returning to the Eden of my childhood in order to provide a concrete example of what I've just sketched out.

It was one of those oppressively hot afternoons when prudent people stay indoors. Any outside chores needing attention had been wrapped up early in the morning, making the neighborhood strangely deserted before lunchtime had even arrived. On another day, we kids might have spent the afternoon digging a hole big enough to hold us all within its earthy cool embrace. We might have perched ourselves in the shaded arms of that welcoming box elder tree just beyond our garden gate or messed around in the vicinity of the drainage ditch threading its way between the birch trees and the climbing oaks. Heaven forbid, we might have even stayed indoors—perhaps begging our way into the home of the older girl down the street, that we might marvel at the shoebox full of quartz crystals she kept tucked away in the coolness of her basement. On this day, however, having been left to my own devices, I proceeded to do what I did best. I unlatched the backyard gate and started walking.

Now, children don't really *take* walks, do they? *Taking* walks is something that we adults do, with a destination, route, and a certain pace in mind—not to mention a reason and many thoughts to entertain us along the way. Children, though, *become* their walks, completely and effortlessly integrating their body and mind with the environment. Such is the wisdom of children.

Thus, I became my walk, living out the reality that there was nothing else to do. I hopped the drainage ditch and skirted the backs of three yards, stopping to look at the cucumbers growing through the chain-link fence of a fourth before veering into the Nursery's interior. It was stifling, still, and silent, save for the crackling sound of a grasshopper's wings as it half leaped and half flew up the path in front of me or the rustling of a field sparrow flitting about in the underbrush off to the side.

There would be days, long after my fall, when I would associate such sweltering solitude with loneliness, sadness, or boredom. On this day, however, I simply settled into that which was, feeling whatever was without trying to name it, explain it, or change it. Yes, I was alone, and nothing much was happening. But by becoming as still and silent as my surroundings, any thoughts of a world that I otherwise might have wished for failed to arise. And in the absence of such thoughts to distract me, the world right in front of me proceeded to reveal itself in all its glory. Streams of red bugs made their way up and down the weed stalks. A cabbage butterfly danced on the humid air. A box turtle crunched slowly through the leaf litter beneath a cluster of saplings. A spider waited, as if dead, in the middle of its web.

With curiosity and wonder, I observed my world in all its varied abundance. It was a world of fruit and flower, root and stalk and leaf. It slithered, crawled, swam, and flew. It was sky above, and earth below. It was sticky and resiny, and soft and smooth. It was sweet and fragrant, and dry and dusty. It was more ways to be than could possibly be imagined—each one unique and each one part of all the others.

I would have loved to have stayed in that world forever. But just as everything creates time in its own way, I had my time as well. Whether prompted by thirst, hunger, or fatigue, I was eventually drawn back home, there to rest and ready myself for the evening. For sweltering summer days have their time too, as did everyone who'd bided their time in the shadows all day long.

Once dinner was over and the setting sun took with it the sweltering heat, the neighborhood came alive again as if it were greeting a brand-new morning. The adults returned to working in their gardens, hosing down their concrete driveways, or sitting on their porches talking. And we children took to riding our bikes up and down the street and sidewalks, ducking in and out of driveways, and chasing each other in intermittent bursts of activity.

With twilight deepening and the air growing cooler, our play reached heightened levels of immediacy. Cicadas droned and fireflies blinked, and mothers one by one took to calling my playmates home. Soon mine would be calling me home as well. How should I spend what little time remained? Should I ride the trails that I'd just walked that afternoon, this time in near darkness? I'd never done that before, but it suddenly seemed like the most important thing I could do. I wheeled my bike out the back gate and into the strangely familiar unknown.

I picked up speed between the birches and white cedars, and by the time I passed the sinkhole, I was riding like the wind. I crossed the clearing and turned onto the road heading down from Gerhardt mansion, with bats tracing spastic circles overhead and fireflies flickering like tea lights all around. I knew the path by heart, every dip and turn and root. But riding in near darkness was brand-new to me, and my heart was pounding in my chest. Then,

27

as I passed the thorny grove of honey locust trees standing like a shadowy council of elders, the trail became as I'd never known before. It somehow knew me and awaited my arrival at every turn. The trees and underbrush and rocks and grass seemed to reach out to me from darkness as I passed.

I'd never felt fear in the Nursery before, except for when I climbed too high up into one of the oak trees or when I almost got stuck up on the barn roof. It took me by surprise. At the beginning of my ride, I'd raced the wind filled with the sheer joy of being alive, but now I turned the pedals furiously just to keep from being seen until I'd already flown past. Onward through the darkness I raced, with the trail twisting and dipping and launching me into the air, catching me and launching me again and again, until my neighborhood, my family, my warm bath and soft bed finally caught me one last time. And as I nodded off to sleep, I knew that there was something about that ride that I would never ever forget.

# Chapter 3: Our Journey Home

By the time we settle into adulthood, we've long since "recovered" from the fall from grace as I've been speaking of it. We've grown accustomed to the separation accompanying what is generally considered healthy ego development and individuation. But that doesn't mean that all is well. It simply means that we're surviving. Yes, and some of us manage to survive quite well, sufficiently desensitized to our separation such that we never think anything is amiss. Others of us are not so "lucky." We end up becoming all too aware over the course of our adult lives of the negative aspects of our separation.

This separation means different things to different people. That I've so liberally invoked the metaphor of a fall from grace will surely have many from the Judeo-Christian traditions thinking in terms of separation from God. In fact, sin is sometimes defined in precisely this way. But we might also think of being separated from our *true self*, the purest and freest essence of being that we might realize. Still others might think in terms of separation from the natural order of life itself. Each of these ways of thinking about separation has something worthwhile to add to the discussion.

What then do we do once we've realized our separation? Must we content ourselves with lives of exile, or can we find our way back home again? Religion offers hope in this regard. Unfortunately, though, we too often view the journey back to wholeness in terms of intellectual or spiritual attainment, or as movement toward a more perfect self or way of behaving. In other words, we presume that the solution to the problem caused by the development of an inordinately strong sense of self is to be found in the enhancement, perfection, or refinement of the very self that causes difficulty in the first place. What I offer in these pages is an invitation to experience anew whatever spiritual practice we might be engaged in. But instead of thinking in terms of movement toward something new and shiny and different, let's try thinking of spiritual practice as a process of remembering that which we already know.

Consider, for instance, the Buddha's journey of awakening. After renouncing his birthright as future leader of the Shakya clan, the man first known as Siddhartha Gautama took leave of his princely existence in order to become a mendicant holy man. He began wandering the Ganges watershed, living off the fruit of the forest and begging in the villages through which he passed. He learned from various teachers along the way how to reach ever deeper stages of meditative absorption. Notwithstanding such expert instruction, however, Siddhartha Gautama remained unsatisfied with the fruits of his quest. His years of extreme ascetic practice had left him perilously weak and depleted but apparently no closer to his goal.

Near death, he recalled how, as a child, he would accompany the royal family and its entourage out to the annual plowing festival. He remembered his nurses getting so caught up in the festivities that they wandered off, leaving him alone in the shade of a rose apple tree. Left to his own devices, he settled spontaneously into a state of meditative absorption that he would only "learn" much later. Inspired by his recollection of that which he already knew, and the timely sustenance offered by a kind passerby, the future Buddha regained his strength and commenced to sitting with newfound insight and determination.

Consider also the story told in the Gospels of an incident that occurred during Jesus's teaching. People began bringing their children to him in order that he might bless them. The disciples tried to keep them away, of course, perhaps thinking that children would only distract Jesus from the teaching of important truths. But Jesus knew otherwise. "Allow the little children to come to me!" he said. "Don't forbid them, for God's Kingdom belongs to such as these. Most certainly I tell you, whoever will not receive God's Kingdom like a little child, he will in no way enter into it."[4]

What are we to make of these two stories? Are they unrelated tales that merely add a bit of color to the overarching messages of these two great teachers, or are these stories central to their respective teachings and, in fact, related? It should come as no surprise that I find the latter to be true!

What is not obvious from the story of the Buddha's awakening is the reality that much of the work he engaged in while navigating those stages of meditative absorption involved letting go of the strong sense of self that we all expend so much energy creating in the years and decades after our fall. Recalling the words of T. S. Elliot, we might say that, after all his years of exploration, the Buddha arrived at the meditative state of his childhood and knew it for the first time.

We tend to forget that part of the Buddha's story, don't we? We're more inclined to think of him as a meditation practitioner of extraordinary accomplishment and a disseminator of a vast store of acquired wisdom. We see in him that which we adults can relate to: the ceaseless quest for the perfection of wisdom and being and the struggle to persevere and overcome. But these are the things we've come to value during and after our fall. The simplicity of a

---

[4] Mark 10:14–15, WEB.

child spontaneously settling into peaceful meditation doesn't make the headlines, does it? It's far too simple!

Jesus, likewise, has a reputation for being the wise answer man. Pose a question to him related to the scriptural dictates of his faith and he would turn it inside out. No riddle could ensnare him. No query could stump him. The Pharisees tried their best, firing questions at him that they might detect the flaws in his logic, the weak spots in his scriptural understanding, or the limits of his spiritual acumen. But Jesus understood that conceptualization and intellectualization cannot bridge the gulf that forms between us and our truest life.

Of course, there will always be a need for critical thinking, logic, and conceptualization. But we also need to set these aside on a regular basis in order to simply be—whether in meditation, silent prayer, or in doing that which makes us feel most naturally alive. Regardless of how we welcome it into our lives, simply being encompasses bridging, healing, overcoming, or transcending the sense of separation that we've come to experience in the wake of our fall.

I spoke earlier of how we acclimate to our separation, at times so completely that we don't even realize anything is wrong for the remainder of our days. We fill our lives with work, recreation, family, and friends—perhaps quite contentedly so—without ever realizing that something is awry. Siddhartha Gautama was living in the lap of luxury when he finally realized that he'd been sleepwalking through his days. Eventually, though, he woke up to his (our) separation so completely that people began referring to him as the Buddha, the Awakened One. Jesus, likewise, was all too aware of our separation. Whether by divine birth or prayerful reflection, he was awakened to something that he and his followers spoke of as the Kingdom of God, that place of truest life from which we become separated.

Such talk of separation must resonate with you on at least some level if you've made it with me this far. Consider that a blessing! For there's little I or anyone else can do for one who is asleep and wishes to remain so. It will take the vicissitudes of life to wrest them from their slumber—or not, as the case may be. The rest of us, having opened our eyes and begun to yawn and stretch a little bit, already know that eerie sense of having had a bad dream that we just can't shake off even in the brightest daylight.

Perhaps we feel as though life is passing us by. Mired in duties and responsibilities, disconnected from our activity, we stumble from one day to the next. Sure enough, there are joys along the way, but they rush past so quickly that we only seem to savor them in hindsight. Maybe things haven't fallen into place like we always thought they would; or if they have, perhaps we have this strange feeling that something more important lies just beyond our grasp. We might feel as though some truer version of who we are is carrying on in a parallel universe somewhere while we, the luckless twin, tarry on in this one. Even darker is when thoughts of meaninglessness begin to creep into our consciousness. What is all this leading up to? Does it mean anything at all? At times, it can feel as though there's no bottom to the abyss into which we fall.

On the other hand, perhaps life is going quite well. We've found meaningful work that rewards us and affords us plenty of free time to spend with family and friends. We've created at least a reasonable approximation to the lives of the rich and famous that are celebrated everywhere we look. Nonetheless, we just can't seem to shake the feeling that we've been lucky, that our good fortune could change at any moment if we were to lose our job or if some accident or illness were to befall us or a loved one. The recognition that everything we know and love could be taken from us in an instant gnaws away at the sense of well-being we might otherwise enjoy. It has us living at arm's length from everything we most care about. We live in relative paradise, and yet we live in fear. And all the while the clock just keeps ticking on our lives.

Anxiety such as this has been with us since the fall—since the emergence of self-awareness out of the pre-dawn mist of prehistoric time. We modern technological humans are simply the first to harbor expectations that life should be free of such concerns. Whereas we used to only have enough to eat when the hunt or the harvest went well, now we expect to be able to buy whatever we desire at the local grocery store at any time of the day or night. Whereas we used to have to settle for whatever work was available in the nearby towns and fields, now we expect to do whatever suits our fancy in order to make a living. And though we used to take for granted that people get sick and die from illnesses over which we have no control, now we expect a cure for every diagnosis that we or a loved one might be given. There is a tacit expectation in our modern technological world that we will enjoy good health, material abundance, and meaningful contentment throughout our many years. Unfortunately, the reality that these expectations so often go unmet only adds to our anxiety. Why can't life simply unfold as it *should*?

Modern technological civilization has advanced to the point where we can realistically imagine a utopian existence here on earth. If only we could calibrate our systems and processes appropriately! Ironically, though, just as technology has advanced to the point of our being able to envision such a possibility, the byproducts and unintended consequences generated by the creation of the proto-utopian civilization in which we presently live threaten to undermine whatever gains technology might afford us. Lifestyle improvements bring new diseases to the fore, even as we *should* be able to cure them. Nuclear technology threatens to annihilate life on earth, even as it *should* be providing us with energy that's "too cheap to meter." Fossil fuel use is warming the planet and threatening our very existence, even as it *should* be providing us with freedom, leisure, and a bounty of cheap goods. Advances in information technology are making us captive in an endlessly upgrading world of applications, platforms, and products, even as they *should* be making our lives so much richer and more efficient.

When I think of the trust that we modern humans place in technology, the blind adherence with which we follow the path of technological advancement, I can't help but think of moths circling the scorching hot bulb of a porchlight on a summer's eve. You see, evolution provided the moth the ability to navigate using relatively faint moonlight. But an evolutionary solution millions of years in the making was disrupted in an instant by the invention of the electric light. Suddenly, with respect to evolutionary time, the world became filled with millions upon millions of false moons— each one promising guidance but providing only disorientation and scorching heat instead.

We humans have evolved an absolute dependence on technology, and for the most part, it hasn't let us down. It's allowed us to hunt big game animals for food and clothing. It's allowed us to farm and preserve what we grow. It's allowed us to build machines that increase our production output, thereby bringing abundance and a higher standard of living to more people than ever before. It's allowed us to cure disease and heal the injured. Given all that technology has done for us, how could we not be predisposed to seek answers to our problems in the promise of its continued advancement?

"You may freely eat of every tree of the garden," our mythical forebears were told, "but you shall not eat of the tree of the

37

knowledge of good and evil; for in the day that you eat of it, you will surely die." Perhaps the advancement of modern technology, more than any other human pursuit, tests the limits of our ability to discern good and evil. So alluring is the power that it yields, and so difficult is it to foresee the ultimate consequences of its use. If only we could just "wake up" and learn to distinguish when we're using technology for unqualified good and when we're setting ourselves up for a falling domino-like sequence of unintended consequences. This is human existence after the fall. This is the result of our ever-increasing self-awareness—the one who knows becoming the one who knows that he knows.

Our prehistoric forebears lived much as described in the legend of the Garden of Eden—wandering the forest unclothed, gathering its bounty, and living without concern for the possible trials of the morrow. After the fall, though, humans felt left to their own devices. The bounty of the forest was no longer enough. Self-awareness brought with it concerns about the future and the sufficiency of what the forest could provide. The natural world could no longer be trusted to provide. We felt compelled to help it along.

We can imagine the advent of agriculture occurring quite gradually. The seasonal return of hunter-gatherers to those places where nuts, fruits, and roots were previously found likely came to encompass watering and "weeding" them as well in order to help them reach maturity. Such watchfulness must have quite naturally grown to include planting seeds in other suitable areas and tending them with increasing frequency. From there it would have been just one more step for those early humans to cut down areas of forest in order to make more room for the plants that they preferred to eat. Such an investment must have made it difficult to leave those fields behind in order to wander elsewhere in search of food. Better to stay and watch over the crops so that another tribe didn't come in and reap the fruits of their labor!

The authors of the Genesis story must have sensed that their reliance on agriculture was a sign of their fallen state. An almost palpable sense of separation is present in their imagining of what God said to that first man and woman in the wake of their transgression. "[T]he ground is cursed for your sake," they were told. "You will eat from it with much labor all the days of your life. It will yield thorns and thistles to you; and you will eat the herb of the field. By the sweat of your face will you eat bread until you return to the ground ..."[5] Not quite the image of bucolic country living, is it? Perhaps the disparity between that early description of agriculture and the romantic imaginings we might have of it today is a testament to our acclimation to the reality of our separation— acclimation fostered by advances in technology, of course.

These biblical ancestors thought of the human predicament as cursed. The Buddha, similarly, described it as one of suffering—

---

[5] Genesis 3:17–19, WEB.

inherently unsatisfactory, rarely remaining as we might wish quite long enough, and remaining contrary to our wishes for far too long. What then are we to do? Shall we double down on efforts to ensure that everything complies with our wishes? Shall we use every technological tool at our disposal to bolster our chance of survival over that of all others? This seems to be the path that we've walked throughout human history. We've even managed to develop the technology of genetic manipulation in order to prune the tree of life itself and bend its branches to suit our wishes. Has God grown tired of guarding the Garden of Eden from which we were banished so long ago?

Our journey back to wholeness is a return to harmonious integration with the earth and all of life. After all, the earth and all of life is the very seamless whole from which we've grown to perceive ourselves separate. But how shall we make things right? The key is to think in terms of going home—returning to that place that we already know, remembering that which we already know. To persist in thinking that our journey toward wholeness is a journey forward to some place yet unknown is to continue as the moth perseveres in circling the porchlight on a summer's eve.

The Buddha's quest for wholeness almost killed him before he realized that he'd already known the way as a child. "God's Kingdom belongs to such as these," Jesus said of the children in his midst. What is it about children that allows them such ready communion with the natural world? What makes them so well-suited for entrance into the Kingdom? We can't go back in time. How then do we reacquaint ourselves with the wisdom of our childhood even as we continue to fulfill our adult responsibilities? I'll begin the next chapter with precisely this question in mind.

# Chapter 4: Our Place

Included in the assortment of Christmas ornaments that my family unpacked each holiday season was a set of six sturdy aluminum foil snowflakes in those anodized metal colorings now so familiar to us all: blue, green, red, violet, silver, and gold. They unfolded from the flatness of their latent state into eight-pointed wonders for which I took personal responsibility. Perhaps because of their size—they were about as big around as dinner plates— they usually ended up becoming my personal bedroom decorations. I'd climb up on the stepladder and attach their strings to the plaster ceiling with asterisks of masking tape that occasionally required a supplemental strip or two over the course of the holiday season.

I liked to watch them as I fell asleep. They'd spin one way when the furnace kicked on and then gradually unwind once it kicked off again, over and over again. I recall my parents having a holiday gathering one time that lasted much longer into the evening after I'd gone to bed. Light from the living room filtered into the hallway and underneath my bedroom door to set those snowflakes flickering as they spun. Murmuring, likewise, filtered in to where I lay, making me feel warm, cozy, cared for, and protected. I had a place. All was as it should be. And as I drifted off to sleep that evening, I likely settled into a state of mind not too far removed from that oceanic state of undifferentiated oneness that a contented infant might enjoy while lying in her crib watching a brightly colored mobile spinning slowly above her head.

Childhood has the potential to foster feelings of security and belonging unlike any we will ever experience. When else but during childhood do we feel as though a place has been created for us alone or that people who are so much wiser and more powerful are watching over us and lovingly considering our every need? Oh, if we could only carry those peaceful feelings into adulthood! The innocence of childhood can't last forever though. And our parents can't be there for us forever either. Besides, we eventually come to realize that they're not as smart or strong as we'd once thought, despite their loving us much more than we could know.

It's understandable that some would want to keep these feelings alive for as long as possible by maintaining belief in a personal and parental God—a beneficent, omniscient, and omnipotent being. If we play well the role of the obedient child, then surely God will continue to play the role of watchful guardian, won't He? But life doesn't always proceed as we would like. Bad things happen even to the obedient. We might be inclined then to reason that God is teaching us a well-deserved lesson—guiding us along as a caring, albeit stern, parent might do.

There are times, however, when innocence and goodness are met with such brutality and injustice that no amount of rationalization can bring us to accept it as being part of God's grand plan. Child victims of war, disease, starvation, and abuse— these all-too-common realities strain to the breaking point our belief in a beneficent and omnipotent God, just as our belief in the infallibility of our parents was eventually strained to the breaking point. We might then be tempted to peel away our idea of a personal God from the harsh realities all around us. We might declare that he still loves us even as he foregoes interceding in the injustices wrought by a world ostensibly of his creation. In this way, we might continue feeling loved for the remainder of our days. And with that sense of love might come a modicum of peace. But the absolute sense of security that we enjoyed in childhood will remain forever in our past. The potential for injustice will always be right around the corner. Crime, disease, financial hardship, disaster, and accident will always be waiting in the wings.

How then do we reacquaint ourselves with the wisdom of our childhood—the wisdom that allowed us to settle unhesitatingly into that calm sense of well-being? Of course, you may question my use of the word *wisdom* here. Perhaps the aphorism that ignorance is bliss is more appropriate from your point of view? Yes, we were ignorant of our parents' inability to truly keep us as safe and sound as we thought we were. We were ignorant of all the ways that our world could come crashing down around us. Alright then, let's step back and explore the nature of that ignorance.

Before the age of twelve or so, children are unable to engage in deeply abstract or hypothetical thought. We think of the world in mostly concrete terms. Our world is what we can apprehend with our senses, and life takes place primarily in the here and now. The finality of death is beyond our comprehension. Selfhood, likewise, is a concept not fully grasped. Think of how a young child, if pressed, might describe herself: "My name is Amy. I'm five years old. I have a dog named Charlie. I like peanut butter and jelly. I like to draw and read books." It's only after the emergence of self-awareness that we come to possess well-developed answers to the questions of who we are, what we're here for, and where we go when we die. The funny thing is, though, despite our answers becoming more and more developed and articulate as we grow older, they are not necessarily any more accurate. Perhaps they're even less so!

Socrates was wise because he knew full well the nature of his ignorance. This wisdom of not knowing is something that adepts of the Zen tradition are quite familiar with. In order to really see in the "Zen" sense, one must let go of words, concepts, and ideas regarding the so-called knower and the known. Only then can real seeing take place. This abandonment of conceptualization extends even to that which we take most for granted—ourselves. The Zen monk, Bodhidharma, for instance, was once asked who he was by the emperor of his day. Bodhidharma famously replied that he didn't know!

Rooted in techniques of Buddhist meditation, mindfulness practice has shown great promise in the treatment of anxiety, depression, chronic pain, addiction, and so forth. It's effective because it gets us back into our body and out of that place where the real suffering takes place—our head. When we're more in tune with our body, focusing on our breath or the coming and going of bodily sensations, we're not worrying about the future or regretting the past; we're simply present in this moment, living out the reality of our existence, much like a child.

Some of the most profound wisdom we can live by urges us to be less sure of what we know, to loosen our iron grip on our sense of self, and to live more fully in the here and now, away from the schemes and concerns that so consume us. In this way, the blissful ignorance (innocence) of our childhood is actually an expression of embodied wisdom—that which we already know.

Lest anyone be confused by what I'm saying, I'm not advocating that we eschew all abstract thought and conceptualization in order to regress to some idealized childhood state. We're adults now and we must stand right where we are and keep on living, however fallen we may be. We need to think clearly

47

and deeply from time to time, and our ability to do so should be nurtured and celebrated. Ideally, we might come to know our minds so well that we're able to use them as an artisan uses his or her collection of tools. When it is skillful and appropriate to chisel away on something, then we do so. When it is skillful and appropriate to refrain from chiseling away on anything, then we refrain from doing so.

Can we ever again know the feelings of security and belonging that we hopefully knew at least at one time as a child? Can we use our minds so skillfully as to dispense with all our unproductive mentation, from the mundane to even the deepest existential ponderings? And what if we do? Will we then lose some of what makes us human? Or will we once more become acquainted with the reality of our truest life?

The suburban neighborhood that I live in has sizable populations of the usual squirrels, rabbits, and birds. Add to that short list all the voles, moles, possums, raccoons, field mice, owls, toads, and snakes that at least make an appearance from time, and we have quite an inventory of fauna. Despite our living in close proximity, however, it's quite seldom that I get to know any particular animal. Each robin or sparrow that visits the birdbath on any given day looks and acts pretty much like every other robin or sparrow. They don't have much personality in that regard. They rarely display any individuality.

Occasionally, though, I do get to know a particular animal, and through that relationship—fleeting though it may be—I'm afforded a unique view of what it's like to live entirely in the natural world. For instance, there was once a mockingbird that perched in the apple tree outside my bedroom window. Every day at around 4:00 a.m. or so, he would commence singing at the top of his little lungs, making it almost impossible for me to get any quality sleep for the remainder of the morning. Part of me resented that little bird for intruding on "my" space, but another part of me felt as though we were kindred spirits. You see, I was grieving the breakup of my marriage at the time, and sleep was sweet refuge from the pain. But that little bird was also a reminder of the universality of my longing. His song was there in my pain. My pain was there in his song. I'll never forget my deep sadness upon discovering the little pile of white, gray, and black feathers in the grass encircling whatever else was left of him. A cat had gotten him, or perhaps it was a hawk or an owl. Such is the way of the world.

There's a squirrel I've been seeing around the neighborhood for a couple of years now. He only has a stub of a tail anymore, likely the result of some violent altercation that I can only imagine. Almost from the moment I laid eyes on him my curiosity gave way to concern. He walked in strange fashion for a squirrel, and I wondered whether his injuries might be more serious than just the loss of a tail. The passage of time assuaged my concerns though.

The awkwardness of his waddle is apparently due to the absence of a tail to use as balance while hopping around in more squirrel-like fashion. Notwithstanding that fact, he seems as happy as a squirrel can be. If for no other reason than that, my spirits are buoyed every time I happen to see him. And if it should come to pass that I one day find a little tailless carcass around the yard or in the street, I'll certainly shed a quiet tear for him as well.

Most of everything that lives and dies around us does so anonymously. Perhaps that mockingbird lived out virtually the entirety of its life alone, with only his mother and father to care that he'd entered the world and only me to care that he'd left. Perhaps that squirrel, awkward as he might appear, will never find a mate in the survival-of-the-fittest world in which squirrels dwell and therefore never know whatever fulfillment there might be in starting a squirrel family of his own. But notwithstanding the seeming indifference the natural world displays toward the life or death of any one of its own, everything still has its place. Everything belongs. The universe has given rise to each and every being in whatever idiosyncratic glory it might embody; and each and every one of them knows precisely how to be.

It's been this way since the beginning of life on earth—with everything belonging and everything knowing how to be. We humans were no exception, for we too were once of the forest in all its abundance and simplicity. Unfortunately, though, life has become so much more complicated. Where once we knew exactly how to be, now it seems as though we're endlessly thrashing about in the underbrush. We've forgotten that we belong. We've forgotten how to be. We've forgotten that we have enough, that we are enough, and that we know enough. Because of our forgetting, we never seem to rest. And because of our inability to rest, we need to be reminded how to be. "See the birds of the sky," Jesus is reported to have said, "that they don't sow, neither do they reap, nor gather into barns. Your heavenly Father feeds them."[6]

Everything that lives carries within it the wisdom of billions of years of evolution. Therefore, everything that lives embodies trust that it belongs. It has a place. Children embody this trust as well. They enter this world not doubting for an instant that they belong. Sure enough, that trust can be taken from them prematurely if they should happen to be raised in an abusive or dysfunctional household. Even in the best of circumstances, though, whatever trust we have will eventually be lost over the course of our fall. We will begin to sow and reap, and when we do, we will begin to worry about the results. It is for this reason that Jesus continued speaking of the birds of the air, saying: "Which of you, by being anxious, can add one moment to his lifespan?"

I mentioned the story told in the Bhagavad Gita of the conversation between Arjuna and his Lord Krishna. Labor is your

---

[6] Matthew 6:26, WEB.

51

birthright, Krishna affirmed to Arjuna, but the fruits of that labor are not. This teaching is quite contrary to our usual way of thinking about things. We're now so goal-oriented and attached to material reward. We've lost track of the fact that our very existence *is* the work of the universe. We *are* the fruit of billions of years of evolution and countless beings sowing without ever reaping. Countless beings proceeded with their work with the entirety of their being, without any thought of their own enrichment—just as the mockingbird, the tailless squirrel, and the child proceed with their work today.

The wisdom of children includes the trust that they belong and have a place in this world. They neither worry about the day-to-day concerns of how to feed and clothe themselves nor the existential concerns that their parents might be struggling with in silence. Yes, we all eventually find a way to sow and reap, but the mind with which we do so makes all the difference. Will we spend our days worrying about whether we'll ever find a mate with which to share this life, or will we simply sing our song with all the heart we have to give, come what may? Will we bemoan our hindered abilities or circumstances and retreat into a place of psychic poverty, or will we hop throughout our days in tailless glory?

I realize now that this understanding has been with me since I first began exploring the Nursery just beyond our garden gate. I knew just how to be when I was there, without ever needing to be taught. The world unfolded like a flower blossoming in my hands, and I, in turn, blossomed completely into the world. No, my understanding wasn't one that I could articulate as I do now with words and concepts. It was understanding that I embodied. Such is the wisdom of children.

I'd just turned four shortly before construction began on the new house across from ours. Certainly, there would have been some discussion in the preceding months regarding such an exciting addition to our little avenue. In my memory, though, the event descended on us out of the blue. Where once an unassuming parcel of land sat vacant across the street, suddenly a rectangular hole reached deep into the red clay earth. I remember us gathering around it that "first" evening, marveling at the sheerness of its earthen walls, wondering at the speed with which so much work had been done, and solemnly pondering the conclusion of the older brothers down the street that the bulldozer now sitting there idle must have been driven down the ramp carved into the other side of the hole in order for the bottom to be so squared off and tidy.

Yes, it was to be just another house. But when you're four years old and have never before seen a house being built, it *is* a big deal. There was so much to experience and explore: the grooves that the big machine clawed into the earth, the shredded roots of the nearby tree, the forms for the foundation walls, the smells of wet concrete and damp lumber, not to mention the various and sundry nails, brick ties, electrical box knockouts, wire remnants, and all manner of building scraps that one could find scattered around a construction site. I remember watching the men work—at times focusing on the actions of one of them in isolation, at other times having the sense of them swarming about like ants. This is what we do. We build things.

Not long after that groundbreaking, we watched a work crew rip up the little vineyard in which we played hide-and-seek behind the houses at the bottom of our street, this time to make way for an apartment complex with a fancy sounding name. Thus, the excitement of construction was always accompanied by our sadness at the destruction that preceded it. Nonetheless, we were always there in search of opportunity in the transition from one thing to another. When the thoroughfare out in front of that new apartment complex was widened, it exposed a deposit of ellipsoidal limestone concretions that we were certain must be fossilized dinosaur eggs worth toiling away day after day to unearth. When the road graders tore through the forested hillside bordering the creek that we'd ride our bikes to, they also allowed us to discover a vine-draped tree from which we could swing out high over the emerging roadbed. And when the new highway carved its way through the limestone bedrock underlying the rolling terrain of our ever-expanding domain, it also afforded us endless hours of fossil hunting amongst the newly exposed outcroppings.

It was only later that my burgeoning adult mind came to associate the construction in and around my old neighborhood with something more insidious and foreboding. Whereas my child's mind simply saw those changes as being part of the natural order—we build things—my adult mind can't help but think we're lost and out of control. We've fallen. I've fallen. We've lost our ability to accept the sufficient bounty of the forest. And I've lost the ability to accept that our human activity is part of the natural order from which we arose.

Earlier, I described a group of turtles sunning themselves contentedly amidst the flotsam of an urban waterway. They were as accepting of the trash in their midst as we children were of the various destructive changes occurring in and around our little neighborhood. We were no more in control of what happened in our environment than the turtles were in control of theirs. We entertained no thoughts of banding together and taking action to put a stop to the encroachment of progress on our areas of play. We harbored no ill will toward "greedy" developers or "pillagers" of the earth's natural resources. No, the wisdom that we embodied as children manifested, at least in part, as complete acceptance of that over which we had no control.

Acceptance comes only grudgingly at times—as in the wake of a bitter and losing battle that ultimately ends with our surrender. The acceptance of children, however, is so complete that it comes without any internal struggle whatsoever. It precedes all judgments as to what is good or bad, right or wrong.

*Xinxin Ming*[7] is a classic Zen poem that touches on this point. Translations vary widely, but some variation of *faith* or *trust* in *mind* seems to reasonably capture the title's meaning. *Xinxin Ming* succinctly describes the predicament of the self-aware individual in its first few lines:

> *The nature of reality is unobscured*
> *As long as one refrains from making judgments.*
> *Begin to make distinctions, however,*
> *And heaven becomes cleaved from earth.*

The making of distinctions is precisely what began in that legendary Garden of Eden all those many years ago. Heaven was thenceforth cleaved from earth and we humans began to hold ourselves captive with the very chains of our own distinctions. The irony of our predicament is that our burgeoning self-awareness— the self-awareness that prompts us to make self-centered distinctions that cleave us from the natural order of things— eventually leads us as well to the realization of our fallen state, to an awareness of the unnaturalness of our ways. This irony is

---

[7] Authorship of this poem is generally attributed to Sengcan, the third great Ch'an (Zen) teacher, Bodhidharma being the first.

present in the *Xinxin Ming*—the irony of our distinguishing between going through life making distinctions and going through life without!

We humans and our self-serving distinctions have certainly created a fair number of problems that can't be resolved simply by refraining from making distinctions from this point forward. What we can do, however, is begin making distinctions from a place of greater wisdom and increased acceptance. By getting back in touch with the wisdom of children, we come to realize that we have enough, that we are enough, and that we know enough. We come to have faith once again in the "sufficiency of the forest" that has always sustained us. Yes, we may have to live like those turtles for a while, amidst the flotsam of our own creation, but our increasing acceptance of what we truly need will, in time, bring heaven and earth back together again.

I don't recall ever telephoning any of my childhood friends in order to see if they could come out and play—*play* being a word that encompassed everything from actually playing a game of some sort to simply sitting on a sewer lid scratching words and pictures onto the concrete with limestone pebbles. It's not that we didn't know how to use a telephone. It's just that such a device seemed so ill-suited to reaching out to a friend who lived in the same neighborhood. Instead, we strolled down the street and stood outside whatever door they tended to use most. We didn't even knock or use the doorbell. We simply proceeded to call out "Oh…, so-and-so…" in a droning sort of voice that started at a higher pitch and ended with the deepest bass note we could muster. If nobody answered after a few rounds of that, then we simply decided it was time to move on.

It was different with Mark Patrick though. Mark lived with his younger half brother, Joe, in the upstairs unit of a two-family apartment building just beyond Gerhardt mansion. Perhaps I wasn't certain that our neighborhood ritual for calling on a friend was understood by others who didn't live on our tiny lane. Perhaps I wasn't convinced that Mark's parents or those who lived downstairs would appreciate it, never having met any of them. Instead, Mark and I simply met up with each other in the same way that we first met, out there in the Nursery whenever the forces of the universe happened to put us in close proximity.

Mark was a couple of grades ahead of Joe and me, but it was he and I who became the closer friends. We'd met out there in the Nursery, after all, a reality that trumped whatever social conventions might keep kids from other grades from hanging out with each other. In the Nursery, things followed the laws of nature, existing when conditions were appropriate, ceasing to exist when conditions waned. That's what made our friendship so special. But it's also what made it come to an end so abruptly. For at least a couple of summers, though, Mark was my favorite friend to hang out with. We would explore, climb trees, and catch frogs and lizards and such. And we did so as kindred spirits, seemingly born of the natural forces that still swirled out there in the Nursery.

I only visited Mark's apartment on one occasion. His parents weren't home at the time, which may well have been the reason for the invitation. We quietly made our way up a side stairway that bypassed the lower level completely and deposited us onto a landing that led to the back hallway of their apartment. It was a collection of rooms that seemed like a veritable ocean of worn hardwood flooring and white plaster walls. The room that Mark and Joe shared was pretty much empty except for a bunk bed and a stack of books and notebooks sitting on the floor in the opposite corner. The window would have overlooked the baseball diamond and the meadow sloping down beyond its outfield. It was summertime, though, and the leaves on the trees at the back of the house prohibited such an expansive view.

I knew little to nothing about what the rest of Mark's life was like. Nonetheless, I was enchanted by what I perceived as its simplicity. He had the Nursery and a bunk bed from which he could survey it once the leaves fell from the trees. There was no unnecessary stuff or clutter. All was quiet and calm. That was how it seemed to me anyway. In adulthood, I would attend meditation retreats at facilities with quarters more lavishly appointed than those in which Mark and Joe lived. And yet it all seemed so beautifully sufficient.

Living things thrive when conditions are sufficient. A seed needs just the right amount of soil, moisture, and light in order to do what nature intends for it to do, but too much moisture and light can be deadly. Children, likewise, are more nourished by an environment that contains just enough to stimulate their imaginations than they are by one saturated with abundance born of the imaginings of others. Mark and I needed a natural area in which to wander and wonder. That was sufficient for our spiritual well-being. It was sufficient for us to happen upon each other from time to time out there in the Nursery in order that a friendship between us might thrive. It was sufficient for us to share what we had together in the moment instead of getting into stories of whatever else was going on in our lives.

Adults, on the other hand, tend to mistake sufficiency for poverty. "These accommodations are merely sufficient," we might say. "This meal is barely sufficient to satisfy my hunger." To the contrary, sufficiency is well worth paying attention to. It's what stands between existence and nonexistence. It's what underlies the Japanese aesthetic of *wabi-sabi*.[8] It is a doorway through which a very special quality of awareness may enter. The sufficiency of accommodations during a meditation retreat is precisely what is

---

[8] *Sabi* conveys the essence of something that is old, worn, or obviously repaired. *Wabi* refers to the rich inner quality that allows one to be content with or even uplifted by that which is merely sufficient to accomplish a task.

required in order to make such an endeavor worthwhile. The sufficiency of resources during a child's formative years is precisely what nurtures creativity and imagination. Children settle into sufficiency's embrace and proceed to attend to whatever is before them in any given moment. To a child, sufficiency is abundance. It is the adult mind that measures, compares, and casts a wary eye upon it.

# Chapter 5: Our Darkness

Childhood is an idyllic time for many—one of incomparable lightness, wonder, and grace. It's a time of immersion in a natural world from which we've not yet declared ourselves separate and a time of freedom from inordinate concern for self-preservation. Indeed, early childhood is a time of freedom from the very idea of a self in need of preservation in the first place. Self-awareness is present during childhood, of course, having begun to precipitate out of the fundamentally fluid nature of human consciousness from the moment we first open our eyes. But it has not yet formed into the fragile sense of selfhood that we adults carry around like a piece of priceless crystal for the remainder of our lives.

But childhood can also be a dark and dangerous time. For some, whatever light may shine must peek through the glorious windows that open up between bursts of gunfire and falling bombs. For others, wonder is a luxury they can scarcely afford in a world where the struggle for self-preservation begins the moment they're old enough to beg on a bustling street corner or scavenge for food in the local dump. For still others, the blossom of childhood grace can't help but wither, rooted as it is in soil made barren by physical or emotional abuse. Thankfully, though, the darkness doesn't usually fall so quickly nor is it so extreme when it does. It arrives incrementally as the already fallen adult world beckons with ever-increasing insistence.

I was raised within the reasonably secure environs of a middle-class neighborhood. I recall learning for the very first time that there are burglars "out there" in the world that break into homes and take things. Most of the time they wait until everyone is away, but every now and then they break in when someone is still at home. Such an awakening to the darker realities of the world might seem rather quaint from our already fallen perspective. Imagine, however, what it's like for a child to suddenly learn that the world is not as safe as he or she has come to believe. In fact, it can be a downright scary place. I still recall the recurring nightmare that followed on the heels of my brand-new awareness of this fact: Someone was standing in the shadows outside my bedroom window, working with some sort of tool to pry it open and climb inside. He knew I was there, but he didn't care. He wanted something of mine, and he was going to take it.

It wasn't long thereafter that the pet beagle of the two brothers down the street was said to be missing. Sugarfoot liked to roam the

Nursery on her own at times, just as I did. This time, though, she hadn't returned. "Has Sugarfoot come home," we'd ask whenever we saw one of the brothers, not realizing that they were keeping a terrible secret. One day, however, our persistence broke down their resolve to keep bad news from our impressionable ears. Sugarfoot had been found dead with an arrow sticking out of her body somewhere out there in the Nursery. It was reckoned that the perpetrator must have been out there practicing with their bow and just couldn't resist a moving target. Yes, we were old enough to be aware of the hunting and killing of animals for food, but this was Sugarfoot! And she'd been used for nothing more than target practice!

Given all the hardship in the world today, some readers may have little patience for such tales of innocence lost. We all must learn the ways of the world sooner or later, mustn't we? It's dangerous out there, and it would be irresponsible if we were to let our children grow up without learning of the potential dangers that await. Unfortunately, this is also how our self-awareness further crystallizes into something brittle and fragile. For along with our newfound realization that there are forces "out there" that can do us harm "in here" comes the investment of psychic energy into the creation and maintenance of a stronger and stronger boundary between the two. Thus, the pace of our fall begins to quicken.

Some may wonder whether I'm advocating that children be raised in protective cocoons until such time as we push them out into a dangerous world without any tools or defenses. No, we're a fallen species, and we've inherited a fallen world. Even as we wake up to the harm caused by an overdeveloped sense of self, we must find ways to ease our children into a world fraught with many dangers. But that doesn't mean we should "throw them to the wolves." It means that we might best nurture them by finding ways to keep them from falling as hard or far or fast as we have fallen. And they, in turn, might be able to do so for their children. It may take generations for us to redeem ourselves as a species. In the meantime, though, we've got to gain a better understanding of the nature of our own fall.

In another of my childhood nightmares, fierce dinosaurs wreaked havoc just beyond the Nursery's eastern boundary— smashing homes and crashing through trees. It must have been deafening for those in the midst of it, given that the roaring and screeching woke me from slumber tucked so far away. Hopefully, they'd stop before they got to the Nursery and our little neighborhood on just the other side. Or maybe they'd veer in another direction, like a storm blown by the winds of its own fury.

One might presume that such a dream must have been inspired by a premature viewing of a Godzilla movie or something. On the contrary, television viewing for us kids was tightly controlled. Such scary movies would have been off limits at the time. I'm inclined to think that what inspired my nightmare was what inspired Godzilla's creator in the first place: a conflation of the erstwhile reality of dinosaurs with the present-day reality of a natural order thrown off kilter by the actions of humankind. No, I didn't yet know of the nightmare of nuclear radiation. But I was learning about the "terrible lizards" of long ago, and I was learning of the destructive power that can be let loose in the here and now. I'd seen with my own eyes how earth movers tear through tree roots and gouge deep into the earth. I'd seen our vineyard playground mangled beneath their tracks. Our beloved realm could be plowed under at any time. It wasn't really ours anyway. The Gerhardts owned it and could do with it as they pleased. It was all just too troubling to contemplate.

Sure, I was a sensitive child. But was I more sensitive than any other? Perhaps I simply recall with greater clarity my burgeoning awareness of the reality of "progress" and the destructive potential inherent in even its most ordinary endeavors. And that was before I'd become aware of the Vietnam War lurking just over my horizon. Yes, the so-called civilized world was truly frightening. Civility was but a mask behind which lurked its horror. Nothing was sacred. Nothing was inviolable. Nothing could be counted on to ever stay the same. I could only count on myself.


I've already mentioned the abundance of ponds out there in the Nursery—tabletop-sized holes left behind after the occasional harvest of a shrub or sapling, deep enough to hold rainwater throughout all but the driest of summers. In Gerhardt Gardens' heyday, the workers likely filled those holes with new plantings as soon as the space became available. During my tenure, though, they were left to grow wilder and wilder with each passing season.

I got to know those ponds well. Given their number and distribution, they could be encountered on virtually any random stroll. But the fact that they were frequently occupied by multitudes of croaking frogs made any one of them an attractive destination in its own right. I'd sit quietly beside one of them until whatever life was in the vicinity either got used to my presence or forgot it, as the case may have been. Birds returned. Water striders commenced again their back-and-forth maneuvering. Dragonflies flitted in to hover above the water or light upon the weed stems on the periphery. And the frogs began anew their croaking chorus.

When I'd visit one of those ponds with a friend, however, we were much more likely to challenge ourselves with catching a few of those frogs rather than being content with merely watching and listening to them. But this required a fair amount of stillness as well, albeit of a more intentional nature. For in addition to being composed and silent, frog-catching demands that you remain watchful for signs of movement in the shadows and amongst the weeds. You must be prepared to move quickly and precisely in order to scoop up your quarry on the very first try. Second chances only come after an appreciable length of time has elapsed.

But even this more intrusive activity was born of a sense of wonder. We took time to examine our prey. We'd peer into their eyes and watch them breathe for a time within our snug grasp before plopping them into a cider jug or something for safekeeping until the hunt was over. Doing so kept us from pursuing to exhaustion some hapless individual that might otherwise have been caught repeatedly. Sadly, though, our activity did one day stray far from the realm of wonder to plunge us deep into the abyss of self-indulgence. It began innocently enough, but by the time our ugly work had run its course it was as if a mirror had been thrust in front of my face to reveal the horror of what I'd become—wounded, separate, and fallen.

It was the height of summer when Mark Patrick and I set up shop beside a pair of adjacent ponds and proceeded to practice the skills that we'd learned. Something was different this time though. Competitiveness crackled in the air between us, informing our play with disorienting intensity. Whereas in times past we'd engaged with a sense of camaraderie this activity that we both enjoyed, now we measured ourselves one against the other. Whereas previously we'd taken the time to get to know every frog, now we deposited them perfunctorily into our respective jars in order to more quickly return to the task at hand. And whereas our work was once the embodiment of our natural sense of wonder, now it was but a contest to be won or lost.

After a time, it became apparent that the competition was drawing to a close by virtue of our having caught nearly every frog there was to catch. All we could really be sure of, though, was that the times in between successive catches were growing longer and longer. How could we know for certain that we'd caught every frog there was? That was the question that prompted us to undertake the greatest engineering feat of our then short lives.

We took to bailing all the water from one pond into the other, catching every last frog in the process—at least in that particular pond. We then dug a trench between the ponds in order to drain the overly full one back into the newly emptied one. By keeping an eye on the trench while doing so, we were able to catch any of the frogs that tried to use it to escape. Then, when the water levels were equal once again, we dammed up the trench and took to bailing the water back into the other pond, catching all the remaining frogs in the process.

It sounds ugly, and it was. The ponds were now just muddy pits with all the surrounding vegetation trampled into oblivion. The water was murky and no longer fit for the frogs that sat patiently in our jugs awaiting freedom. They didn't know that their home had been laid to waste. I felt sick and ashamed. I felt dirtier than my mud-smeared arms and legs could possibly attest. Mark and I emptied the frogs into some other nearby ponds, and then we solemnly parted ways. And as I walked back home alone, the weight of my deed sank with full force onto my shoulders.

I didn't want to go out and play the following day. Returning to the Nursery would only bring me face-to-face once again with my crime. But neither could I erase it from my mind simply by staying away from the scene. It was an even hotter day than the previous one. The solitary window air conditioner in our front room droned loudly, barely keeping at bay the oppressive heat. I lay on the couch beneath it, gazing out at the maple trees in the front yard beginning to sway in the gathering breeze. A storm brewed inside of me. The maples began to soundlessly pitch and bend. A storm brewed outside as well. I couldn't hear it over the air conditioner, but I could see it. The sky was growing dark, as was my mind. The universe was displeased with me. I was no longer part of all that was. I was separate, and it was painful. There was no longer anywhere to go. There was no longer anyplace to be.

At the moment of our human birth, there is no questioning the naturalness of our being. We are each a living, breathing organism arising out of and interacting with this physical world with the totality of our being. But whereas all others in the animal kingdom remain immersed in this natural state for the remainder of their lives, we humans are an altogether different breed. Our neurobiology made possible by millions of years of evolution will eventually give rise to the fully developed self-awareness that makes us stand apart from the natural world. We tend to think of this development in positive terms—perhaps as the dawning of our light of humanness. But there's no denying its negative side, that of our inevitable descent into the fallenness of our fully mature state of being.

Perhaps it's on account of the latter that we so often look back on our childhood days with great nostalgia. We were so much more firmly rooted in the present moment in those days. If not completely carefree, we could at least relinquish those cares with greater ease. We could learn that there are burglars "out there" in one moment, and in the next we could run off and play without a single care in the world. We could see images on the television of a war raging somewhere "out there" in the world, and then we could run on over to a friend's house as if oblivious to the darkness. Sure enough, those concerns would return. But our orientation to the present moment enabled us to more easily return to our fully functioning engagement with the world, our gloriously spontaneous and uninhibited childhood state.

During those most glorious of childhood days, we had just enough self-awareness to keep from tripping over our feet as we ran like the wind down the street. We had just enough self-awareness to know how far up into the tree we could climb without unduly risking an injurious fall. We had just enough self-awareness to keep from burning ourselves on the stove or steering our bikes out into a busy street. Thankfully, though, our burgeoning self-awareness had not yet begun to distract us from full immersion in whatever activity we were engaged in. We'd not yet become inhibited by self-consciousness.

Sooner or later, all children must learn to meet the challenges and dangers of the "outside" world, and we adults would be remiss in not helping them along in that regard. Thus, the list of things to fear keeps growing, in part due to each child's acquisition of a more accurate assessment of an already fallen human world, and in part due to her expanding awareness that there is indeed a self to be harmed and many ways for that harm to be inflicted.

The Buddhist concept of karma makes sense in this regard—not in the sense of some cosmic balance sheet of all the good and bad things we do but in the sense of created patterns of existence and behavior. There is karma that we share with all living things, for instance, such as our need to take from our environment in order to survive. This is the karma expressed by the respective genomes of all living things. There's also karma that only we humans share, such as the "hardwired" neurobiology that gives rise to our self-awareness and the "programmed" karma related to our social mores, myths, and historicity. Similarly, there is the familial karma of our biological heritage intertwined with whatever shared experiences and interpretations might happen to get passed down from generation to generation via story and imitated behavior. There's also the karma that most of us think of—those individually idiosyncratic patterns of thought and behavior, whether unconscious in nature or purposefully replicated.

The children of our Stone Age ancestors had substantially less to learn from their elders than the children of today. Little was required of them in the way of toilet training and personal hygiene. There was no alphabet to learn or multiplication tables to memorize. Learning and work were seamlessly integrated into day-to-day existence, and day-to-day existence was seamlessly integrated into the totality of the natural world, just as it was for any of the other animals of the forest. Sure, there were tools to be made—the flint knapping of spear points and the carving of needles and fishhooks. However, other than a few such notable and uniquely hominid exceptions as these, our Stone Age ancestors hunted in a manner similar to other social predators. They gathered food in a manner similar to other foraging animals. They read the seasons and ranged like other migrating animals. Every action grew out of the reality of the natural world. Just as a bird builds its nest in precise fulfillment of its needs, neither superfluous nor incomplete, so our Stone Age ancestors lived from day to day to day.

How different life is for us modern humans! How insufficient the sufficiency of the forest has become! How insufficient *we* have become! With self-awareness comes the nagging sense that we don't have enough, that we don't know enough, that we aren't capable enough, and that we're lacking and incomplete. This sense of insufficiency and incompleteness is prominent enough to have earned a place in one of the most influential theories of psychological development. Alfred Adler asserts in his theory of individual psychology that it is how the developing child deals with feelings of insufficiency and incompleteness (inferiority) that determines the type of person he or she will become.

While our forebears only eventually came to realize their nakedness back there in that proverbial Garden of Eden, we modern humans come to realize it all too quickly. With nakedness comes shame and fear of the shame that might be. With nakedness comes fear of insufficiency and fear of losing that which we perceive ourselves to have gained. And with nakedness comes scheming in order to secure that which we fear living without. Feelings of nakedness result from our neurobiological karma manifesting self-awareness. This burgeoning self-awareness then becomes manifest within the social milieu in which we are raised. The fears of our parents, neighbors, and nation become our own, often keeping us in our fallen state for the remainder of our days. Such is the nature of our karma.

# Chapter 6: Our Cage

Imagine, if you will, that child of tender years that you once were. Perhaps you're five or six years old. You're visiting relatives or perhaps some of your mother's or father's friends you've never met before. Awkward introductions commence, and at least one of the adults smiles at you and asks you what you want to be when you grow up. Would you have engaged in delighted imaginings, or would you have parroted precocious certainty instead? Would the question have even made any sense to you, or would it have left you feeling downright confused? Count me amongst the confounded.

Oh sure, I engaged in my share of role-playing fun. As most boys did back then, we played cowboys and Indians and other war games. From time to time, I even dressed up in a Batman costume that my mother sewed for me, pretending to be as big and strong and smart as the "real" one on television. By the time Halloween came around, though, more likely than not I wanted to dress up as a hobo.

I'd like to think that this default choice for a Halloween costume foreshadowed my later appreciation of one of the most highly evolved hobos of all time, the Buddha. However, dressing up as a bum *was* fairly popular for young boys back then. Little was required other than grease-penciling a scruffy beard on your face, throwing on one of your father's old flannel shirts, and tying a bundle of rags wrapped in a kerchief to the end of a found stick. Notwithstanding the simplicity and popularity of this particular costume, I can't help thinking that there's something telling about this early desire to be a hobo.

Do I reveal too much of my adult psyche in saying that, whenever I drive by one of those still wild places that exist down in the overgrown culverts alongside the highway or on those odd parcels of land too small or inaccessible to be of much commercial value, I think of sitting there in solitude, perhaps even sitting there all night, the quiet observer that I've been for as long as I can remember. I think I know just a little bit of what it must be like to be a hobo, to feel as though there's little in this so-called civilized world worth belonging to, to feel as though living amidst the truth of those still wild places, as difficult and insecure as that might be, is better than dying slowly amongst the falseness of a fallen world. Did I somehow sense that long ago? Is that what inspired me to dress up as a hobo on those Halloween nights so long ago?

We develop self-awareness so gradually, and ultimately identify with it so completely, that we tend to forget those childhood days when we had very little of it at all. When we ask a child what they want to be when they grow up, we assume that they have a similarly robust and well-defined sense of self as we do, with the same ability to project those aspects of who we think we are into whatever prospective role we might contemplate. But children aren't yet capable of doing this in any meaningful way. They are so innately expert at being precisely what they *are*, with neither effort nor forethought, that the idea of one day *choosing* what they will be is totally foreign to their experience. The world of the child is not yet a collection of puzzle pieces amongst which they must fit. No, their developing capacity for self-awareness has not yet taken up the laser beam of intellect in order to create myriad separate pieces of the world in the first place.

What a child *is* is the totality of everything in their world: their siblings and parents, their friends and neighbors, their home, yard, and neighborhood. Like those urban water turtles, children settle amongst the flotsam and jetsam of this modern world without judgment or separation. They simply are. The world simply is. The two of them are not yet two. The question regarding what they want to be when they grow up intrudes upon their world like a voice calling from some far-off place, warning them: "You live in oneness now, my child. You live without wanting to be anything other than precisely what you are. But that won't last. Someday soon you'll learn to be separate from all that is. Someday soon you must *choose* what you will be."

Yes, this is the way of the world. And we would be remiss if we let our children grow up without contemplating all that is within their power and purview to do and become. The difficulty is that, in doing so, we also foster a sense of separation from all that is. By becoming one thing, we become separate from everything else. In so doing, we lose track of the oneness of our birthright.

Imagine, one more time, that child that you once were. Do you remember running through the woods or down the street, without concern for how fast or far, without concern for the smoothness or clumsiness of your gait? The universe said run, so you did. The entirety of your being said run, so it did. There's simply no arguing with the universe or the entirety of your being, at least not when you're a child. Do you remember drawing, finger painting, or coloring without the question ever entering your mind as to whether you were "good at it" or whether it was a worthwhile pursuit or not? You were alive and fully engaged with the world, without a trace of ambivalence or self-judgment. Sure, we still enjoy such moments in adulthood—less often perhaps, and under circumstances more contrived—like when we're engaged from time to time in a favorite pastime that allows us to "lose ourselves." But what makes childhood such a wondrous time is the fact that we don't yet possess such a strong sense of self to be lost in the first place.

The development of this strong sense of self can be thought of more precisely in terms of the development of two distinct but intertwining psychological realities—one a construct, the other a capacity. Namely, we are in the process of *constructing* our sense of self even as we are developing the *capacity* for reflective awareness of that self. Each requires the other. So, what exactly is going on as we mature and proceed with the construction of this thing that many of us come to believe is even more real than the universe that gives rise to it?

Recall the oceanic state of undifferentiated oneness that I spoke of earlier, that state in which the infant does not yet perceive any separation between self and other. From there, the infant begins to explore his environment. He maps out the physical boundaries between what is "inside," those internal bodily sensations and tactile sensations of pleasure and pain, and what is "outside," that which can be touched without him feeling it. A rudimentary conception of self and other begins to form.

With the development of language skills, this mapping of self and other becomes more refined. We begin to overlook the world's oneness, seeing it instead as a collection of things, each with its own name and set of attributes. The sky is blue. The grass is green. Fish swim. Birds fly. The child, too, has a name and attributes as well. Recall how young Amy described herself in an earlier chapter: "My name is Amy. I'm five years old. I have a dog named Charlie. I like peanut butter and jelly. I like to draw and read books."

Of course, children don't just spontaneously take to cataloguing their attributes. Amy would have required some coaxing in order to create such a description, and further coaxing to relate it. In this way, we all play a role in the construction of a child's sense of self. We are their mentors and their mirrors. Ah, but what harm is there in that? Nobody's telling Amy what or how she should be. Her description simply arises from the reality of her young life, doesn't it? Perhaps. Sooner or later, though, Amy will be introduced to the concept of being good or bad at the things that she does. She'll begin to evaluate how well she reads, draws, and does a whole host of other things. She'll begin to internalize the evaluations of others and include them in her sense of self.

Please don't misunderstand me. Experiences both personal and professional have given me a deep appreciation of the value of our being able to discover what we're good at and what we enjoy and being able to nurture that self-knowledge into a meaningful and rewarding career. And what a difficult process this can be! One rather obvious difficulty arises when what we're good at and what we enjoy end up being two very different things, or when what we're both good at and enjoy is without any appreciable economic value. How then shall we choose our life's work? What criteria shall we use? Less obvious, though no less difficult, is when we confuse our being skilled at something with our enjoyment of it. Perhaps we've come to confuse our enjoyment of the extrinsic reward that we earn for being good at something with our intrinsic enjoyment of it.

A famous tennis champion revealed some years ago that he hated the game, that his father forced him to engage in arduous training from a tender age, and that it was a lonely and joyless pursuit. Consider your reaction to such a revelation. Can you allow yourself to grieve in at least some measure for that child denied the opportunity to discover on his own what the universe wanted of him? Or are you inclined instead to dismiss such psychic turmoil with a shrug? He's now rich, after all, and happily married to another beautiful champion! How bad can life be? Life is complicated like that, with joy and sorrow all tangled up together in whatever package we embody. I can imagine that every one of us has a bittersweet tale to tell of how we came to be what we are in this present day.

I was well along in middle school by the time U.S. involvement in the Vietnam War began winding down. Another student conveyed the news as we were waiting to board the school bus for the ride back home. And as the bus lurched and swayed and deposited us in little clusters here and there, it began to sink in. The nightmare that I'd lived with for so long—that of being plucked from home against my will and dropped into the middle of a jungle firefight—was not to be my reality after all. I was free to dream of a future. I was free to determine what I would be. But the capacity for dreaming is not something that can be turned off and on at will. It atrophies, as muscles do, if not used for too long a time. And so it was that my high school years came and went without any dream of a future taking root within me. Meaning was too difficult to find amongst the myriad pieces of a world that seemed to have shattered from the farthest reaches outside of me to the deepest places inside.

Thankfully, I had my poetry. Poetry allowed me to at least attempt to reconcile my erstwhile sense of seamless integration with that of a brain suddenly overflowing with words glistening like bits of fractured window glass. Even where no other meaning could be found, there was at least that which was inherent in giving voice to my own unique awareness. Unfortunately, though, despite it quite possibly saving my life, poetry was not a very practical skill to take out into the bleak economic climate of those days, especially given the sensibilities of my family of origin. By the time I entered college after a couple of years spent looking for a signpost out there in the fog, there was little for me to do but begin taking coursework in the most marketable subject matter that I recalled being good at—mathematics. No, it wasn't what I truly loved. Not unlike that reluctant tennis champion, however, I parlayed it into a level of financial stability for which I am grateful and which now allows me more congruent pursuits.

It is somewhat ironic then that I would later stumble into a position of providing guidance to those in circumstances not all that different from the one in which I found myself so many years ago. Is it really such a stretch to see the similarity between where I was then and where so many urban youths are today, growing up in neighborhoods too dangerous or too impoverished for dreams to take root, finding meaning in little other than their rhymes?

And what about you? Do you dare trace the twists and turns your life has taken? What if the illusion of the inevitability of the "you" that you've become should end up crashing down around you? Indeed, the longer the universe allows us to bask in the apparent stability of our created selfhood, the more attached we become to the concepts and material trappings that we've used to construct it. Do you dare contemplate what's beneath the façade of the "you" that you've become? Do you dare contemplate the possibility that the mortar holding all of it together is the very fear of nonexistence?

*The nature of reality is unobscured*
*As long as one refrains from making judgments.*
*Begin to make distinctions, however,*
*And heaven becomes cleaved from earth.*

The author of this poem was speaking of Zen practice, but he may well have been referring to what took place in the proverbial Garden of Eden after our forebears tasted the fruit of the tree of the knowledge of good and evil. They began making

85

distinctions, thereby precipitating their estrangement from both the creator and the created. On a deeper level, though, this poem is about the construction of the self as I've been speaking of it here. For the construction of the self is nothing if not an endless series of judgments and distinctions that cleave "us" from everything else. I like this. I don't like that. I want that. I don't want this. I'm good at this. I'm not good at that. This is me. That's not me.

The process of individuation involves the making of distinctions as to who and what we are. By young adulthood, unless some inordinate developmental difficulty has become apparent, we've begun to adopt our various personae and play our various roles. Before long, we've become so used to this thing that we call our self that we can't even imagine it not existing in some way, somehow, somewhere, no matter what. We've also likely adopted certain beliefs regarding afterlives, reincarnation, or heavenly realms—elaborate imaginings that serve to assuage our fear that this thing we expend so much energy to construct and maintain might one day no longer exist. Children, on the other hand, have no need for such beliefs. They've not yet adopted such a strong sense of self, so they don't yet have the same fear of its nonexistence as do we adults.

Unfortunately, the creation of the self brings with it much more than the fear of nonexistence. It brings with it a host of other fears that further constrain the freedom that we once enjoyed. Again, do you remember running through the woods or down the street, without concern for how fast or how far, without concern for the smoothness or clumsiness of your gait? And do you remember how one day it became apparent to you that you *should* be concerned with how fast and how far you can run and the form you display as you do. Or perhaps you decided that you aren't a runner after all. You're "no good" at running, and so you've swore off it until such time as a life-threatening danger might present itself.

And what of the drawing, finger painting, or coloring that you used to love to do without the question ever entering your mind as to whether you were "good at it" or not, or whether it was a worthwhile pursuit or not? Did you end up deciding one day that you weren't really artistic at all and that your time would be better spent engaging in things that you're "good at" rather than not? Or perhaps you decided that you are indeed an artist and, as such, everything that you now create must be worthy of inclusion in your oeuvre. For every act of creation and expression will now be judged in terms of how it impacts your reputation, your product, and your marketability.

These are just a couple of very simple examples, of course. There are countless ways that we allow our ideas of who we are to constrain and confine us. Perhaps you think of yourself as a successful person, so your present assessment that your career has stalled or taken a nosedive has your self-esteem in the gutter. Perhaps you fancy yourself an independent person, so the reality that an illness now makes you so much more dependent on others has you questioning your very self-worth. Perhaps you've always considered yourself an honorable person, so the fact that you just got caught doing something quite to the contrary has you contemplating suicide. Isn't it strange how, after having entered this world with unbounded freedom, we risk departing it within a cage of our very own creation?

What then is your happiness based on? What are the judgments and distinctions that you make in determining whether you're having a bad day or a good one? Come on, you know you make them! Even a hermit living in stark simplicity out in the desert does as much. Watch him try to live in the middle of a noisy and bustling urban sprawl and those criteria will soon become apparent.

What does your cage look like? Is it a professional image from which you dare not stray lest you cease to be taken seriously by clients and colleagues? Is it some concept of beauty versus unattractiveness? Is it a tangle of political beliefs that you can't help but trip over no matter how nimbly you might move? Is it the need to be good? Perhaps it's the need to be bad! Is it a system of doctrinal religious beliefs that keeps you from engaging fully with the very reality of being itself? Is it an image, a fashion, an attitude, or some vague sense of personal progress? Is it some standard of health that you identify with? Perhaps it's sickness that you identify with instead? Is it the idea of being wealthy that captivates you? Do you have some reputation for intelligence, creativity, or expertise that you must uphold at any cost, or do you find sanctuary in mundanity instead? Do you live in a plain box of stability and normalcy, or is it a profusely decorated box screaming wildness and unconventionality that constrains you? And if it should come to pass that you see some truth being spoken here, what will you do? How will you free yourself? I've got an idea. How about returning to that which you already know?

# Chapter 7: Our Fullest Functioning

By the time I entered middle school, life had begun to move much faster than I was used to. Where once we had just one classroom to report to—and the occasional art, music, or gym class to which we were escorted—now we had seven or so places to be on any given day. We had so many books and papers that we needed lockers in which to store them all. But perhaps the most stressful thing about attending a new school was the realization of the passage of time. I really *was* getting older; and getting older meant getting closer to my day of reckoning with that jungle war overseas. It was something that I could almost put out of my mind as long as we were in the same school building year after year. But entering middle school meant I was almost in high school—the last milestone standing between me and the war.

It will probably come as no surprise then that the start of middle school brought with it bouts of anxiety unlike any I'd ever experienced. I'd close my locker door, spin the combination lock, and head off down the hall, only to become gripped by doubt as to whether the door was really locked or not. This feeling grew with each step, accompanied by imaginings of my belongings being strewn up and down the hall by one class bully or another. Finally, I simply had to turn around.

The bullies were something new as well. Sure, there'd been the occasional tussle out on the playground back in grade school. But everyone was about the same size back then. By middle school, however, some of the boys had grown manlier in stature, and a couple of them weren't above showing off their newly acquired status. In retrospect, they were probably dealing with some newfound anxiety of their own, anxiety that could be assuaged at least to some extent by displaying power over another. We were all creating the selves we would one day become.

You would think I'd have gotten used to my new locker after a week or so. To the contrary, my anxiety only grew stronger as the school year wore on. As much as I tried to shrug off my urges to go back and check, all too often I'd end up hurrying back anyway— feigning that I'd forgotten something if anyone happened to be watching. There were times, though, when even my checking didn't make any difference. I'd make it down the hall once again only to wonder whether I'd merely *imagined* that I'd gone back and checked! Maybe I needed to go back and check again, or for the first time, as the case may have been. So, I'd go back and check, trying to be especially mindful as I pulled up on the handle in order to prove once and for all that everything was as it should be.

The cage of the self was closing in around me. Who had control over me? Who was in charge of my mind? Who was I anyway? Was I destined to go through life jerked this way and that by every errant thought or worry? I needed to be stronger and more in control than that. I wouldn't survive otherwise! And so I began to pay closer attention to "my" mind—making sure that I was paying attention when I really needed to do so. I vowed that if I got down the hall and couldn't recall whether I'd been paying attention, then I'd simply let it go. I steeled myself to whatever humiliation might result. If I should return to find my belongings strewn about, then so be it. I was the one in charge of me. Except when I wasn't in charge at all, of course!

It wasn't too long after this period of anxiety that I learned I'd likely not have to fight in that jungle war after all. It would all be over soon. Now, my adult self would no doubt throw a party if, after years of believing otherwise, I were to suddenly learn that I wouldn't have to go off and fight in some terrible war. I might even celebrate each anniversary of that day on which my life was given back to me! As a child, though, my days continued without even a hint of recognition by any of the adults in my life that this was a monumental turning point. Apparently, children were thought to be unaware of the tumult in their midst. Thus, I simply set about putting it all behind me. And, superficially anyway, that really wasn't all that difficult. So much was changing so quickly back then that new concerns simply rushed in to fill the empty space left behind by the departure of my war-related anxiety.

My parents were looking for a new home for us. There were three of us kids by then, and it was becoming obvious that we needed more space. We might even have to move to a different school district, an ominous prospect all by itself. One thing that was certain, though, was that I wouldn't be seeing very much of the Nursery or my neighborhood friends any longer. Sure, I'd be able to visit from time to time on my bike. But that wasn't the same as being able to stand on someone's doorstep calling for them to come outside and play. It wasn't the same as being able to lift the gate latch whenever I needed the Nursery's embrace.

I must have understood on some level how much I'd miss my beloved Nursery. But with so much going on, I suppose I lost track of what was at stake. Perhaps we don't really understand how much our breath means to us, either, until such time as the wind gets knocked out of us and it's no longer there. Besides, some school friends and I had become serious cyclists by then. We'd pedal for miles to explore new places down along the creek, or where the new highway had been blasted through the fossil-rich limestone, or around the old quarry way out beyond the outskirts of town. With so many new places vying for my attention, I'd somehow forgotten that the Nursery *was* me. Sadly, the ensuing months slipped past without my ever going back.

Oh sure, my gaze would wander across that open field sloping down from Gerhardt Gardens every time the school bus carried me past. And I couldn't help but think of it each time I heard a croaking frog or spied a dragonfly. Nevertheless, I kept telling myself I could always return. But then the billboard went up declaring the coming of a new apartment complex. Bright orange survey flags began to appear. And then it happened, what I feared would happen ever since the vineyard got plowed under, the bulldozers and earth graders began doing the same to that which had always been my beloved domain.

I remember the horror and shame that one must feel after putting off visiting an ailing friend only to unexpectedly learn that they've already passed. I'd been in denial thinking that I could always return. No, I wouldn't have to go to war. But after seeing my beloved Nursery become so completely and utterly destroyed, I felt as though I knew just a little bit of what it might be like to live through one. In war, nothing is gained without destruction. In war, nothing matters but the will of the victorious. In war, nothing is sacred. In war, life is valued only in terms of its utility.

Never again will I wander those Nursery trails, climb those glorious oaks, or sit watchful beside those frog ponds. And yet, I go there almost daily in my mind. Something happened back there that made my life what it is today. I was that place. Yes, I *was* that place. Before self-awareness made me stand out from the seamless reality of all that is, I *was* that place. There, I could simply be, without ever having to endeavor to be something.

And what about you? Do such childhood memories visit you from time to time, washing over you like an unexpected wave that quickly recedes? Maybe you purposefully set about plumbing their depths for clues that might point you toward something deeper— be it meaning, healing, wholeness, understanding, or a sense of closure. On the other hand, perhaps you do your level best to keep such memories in their place, locked in a trunk along with all your other bundles of pain and fear, anger and abuse.

Regardless of how pleasant, difficult, or intentional the recollection of our childhood stories may be, revisiting them can help us clarify the nature of our present lives. From them we can glean insight into the genesis of our neuroses and defense mechanisms, thereby diminishing our reactivity in the here and now. They also help us better understand the unfolding of our karma—our created patterns of thought and behavior—thereby allowing us to act with greater freedom in the present. Notwithstanding such insights, however, there is an even more fundamental benefit to examining these stories and recollections: they allow us to take stock of the wisdom that is already ours.

Wisdom awaits our recognition. Wholeness awaits. It simply requires our awareness for it to become known again. Some might find this vaguely reminiscent of psychoanalytic theory, wherein newfound awareness of some previously unconscious conflict allows it to be brought forth to conscious resolution. The difference is that, whereas the goal of psychoanalysis is to bring forth awareness of some forgotten brokenness, what I'm speaking of is our forgotten wholeness.

Let me be clear, though, I'm not advocating that anyone curtail their psychotherapeutic regimen for the sake of celebrating wholeness that they've not yet fully realized. Instead, I hope the insights gleaned from these pages provide more meaningful context for that regimen. We all must "render unto Caesar" to at least some extent. But if we allow ourselves to be judged by the prevailing criteria of this fallen world, then we might indeed conclude that we are broken. Our minds aren't fast enough to keep up with its pace. Our skills aren't valued enough in its ever-changing economy. Its social disconnectedness has us feeling lost and alone. Its stress and fear-inducing realities place undue pressure on our psyches. This is when any so-called "weakness" becomes revealed. However, when viewed within the context of our higher power, our truest self, our Lord, our God, our creator, our source, our ground, our ultimate reality, our Buddha-nature, etc., we are unbroken to this day. We are whole. We need only fully realize that it is so.

It's ironic that after growing tired of playing the "not enough" game that society teaches us to play, after beginning to survey our world for something more meaningful or spiritual, we then risk succumbing to that "not enough" thinking all over again. We study holy books, but our understanding isn't deep enough. We dust off the beliefs of our parents, but our faith just isn't solid enough. We take up yoga or some other health regimen, but our resolve just isn't strong enough. We start to meditate, but our mind just won't calm down enough. We seek guidance from one spiritual "expert" or "holy" individual after another, only to be told that we're not praying enough, or giving enough, or practicing enough, or meditating enough, or studying the holy books enough, or going to worship enough …

Near death after struggling for years with a spiritual practice that just wasn't "good enough," the Buddha recalled spontaneously entering into meditative absorption as a child in the shade of a rose apple tree. It was only after he approached his meditation in that way that he realized his enlightenment. One last time, though, he was tempted to fall into the trap of "not enough." The demon, Mara, so the story goes, demanded of him a witness as to the depth of his enlightenment. The Buddha responded by touching his hand to the earth. He was part of everything. He was enough.

Recall the words of Jesus: "[W]hoever will not receive God's Kingdom like a little child, he will in no way enter into it." Whereas others thought that the children might not be mature enough, intelligent enough, or understanding enough to be in the presence of one so holy, Jesus knew otherwise. It is precisely what the children already know that makes them most receptive to the kingdom of God right here and now.

I'm also not advocating that anyone curtail their existing spiritual practice for the sake of celebrating some newfound wholeness they've not yet fully realized. I simply advocate getting in touch with the wisdom we already have so that we might continue our practice on a more solid foundation and with a more down-to-earth understanding of what we're doing. Toward that end, let's delve into a concept that I've only talked about in passing thus far.

I've referred to the *full functioning* nature of children without providing a formal definition, relying instead on context in order to invest it with adequate meaning. The term has a rich history, though, and I would be remiss if I didn't explore it a bit further. *Full functioning* was first defined by Carl Rogers in order that he might have some objective criteria for determining the psychological and behavioral health of the adult individual. Such criteria could then be used to determine the success of the counseling process or the need for it in the first place.

However, there is a key difference between the way I use the term and the way Rogers uses it. Whereas Rogers speaks of full functioning as a state of being attained by the self-actualized adult, perhaps after having successfully engaged in the process of psychotherapy, I consider it to be the birthright that we unwittingly discard or have taken from us as we mature and engage in the process of constructing our self in this fallen world. The two perspectives are easily reconciled if we remain mindful of the context. Let me take a moment then to review three fundamental attributes that Rogers[9] considers the full functioning individual to possess: *experiential openness, organismic trust,* and an *existential orientation.*

The *experiential openness* that Rogers speaks of does not necessarily involve becoming more receptive to skydiving, ballroom dancing, or what have you, although I suppose such expanded receptivity would not be out of the question. Rather, our return to full functioning encompasses greater freedom from reliance on whatever defense mechanisms we've constructed in order to protect ourselves from that which we deem uncomfortable. Defense mechanisms distort our view of reality in service of the created self. Openness to experience entails a newfound openness to experiencing the world precisely as it is, along with whatever difficult emotions such unprotected awareness might bring forth.

In the classical Freudian sense, defense mechanisms are constructed and invoked by the unconscious mind. In a more general sense, however, we construct ways of looking at the world that tend to bolster our own self-image. An example might be an

---

[9] See, for instance, *On Becoming a Person: A Therapist's View of Psychotherapy.*

individual who enjoys reasonable material abundance protecting himself from the anxiety of seeing others living in poverty by constructing a worldview in which those who work hard are rewarded and those who are lazy go without. This "just world" view protects the holder from having to worry that poverty might befall him despite all his hard work. It also alleviates him of any sense of responsibility that he might otherwise be burdened by regarding helping those who live in poverty.

Children have not yet constructed such defenses. They don't yet have a strong sense of self in need of protection. Sure, a child might recoil from an unfamiliar person or situation, but this is precisely because she greets life without defense. If something frightens her, then it frightens her. She feels no need to justify her fear or create the false impression that she isn't really afraid at all. Her inner feelings and her outer appearance and behavior are congruent. Keeping up appearances that she is cool, fearless, in charge, or unfazed will come later, once she has a self-image to protect.

Another aspect of full functioning is *organismic trust*—trust in one's being, one's gut, one's felt sense or intuition. The full functioning individual trusts himself to assess whatever new situation might present itself and behave accordingly. He doesn't feel any compulsion to follow the herd, to check on how some respected individual might have behaved in a similar situation, or to reflect upon how his actions might be viewed by others. He has confidence in his ability to read situations clearly and accurately, including the ability to read clearly and accurately his own feelings about those situations.

We adults often end up second-guessing ourselves, especially with respect to the various personae we adopt. Since our personae do not necessarily arise from any innate or natural need, we might need to learn the "right way" to behave. Suppose a new corporate manager gets a call from a low-level employee in another department, for example. The new manager might ponder what the corporate culture would have him do. Should he feel honored that he's already being viewed as a valued resource on the corporate team, or should he feel chafed that some underling thought he could just call up the manager of another department without going through the "appropriate" channels? Should he simply return the call, or should he find out who the caller's supervisor is in order to have a chat with him or her?

This is a contrived example, of course, but don't we think along very similar lines much of the time? Which persona am I in this particular case? What are the expectations for someone in this role? How will this look? What will people think of me? We often expend energy trying to figure out how to behave based on our observations of the behavior of others who've adopted the same persona. It's as if we're constantly comparing some cardboard cutout version of ourselves to whatever template exists out there in society for who we think we're supposed to be. The full functioning individual has little need for outside validation of his feelings or actions. He can be himself regardless of the situation. If he is unskilled in some area, then he is unskilled; he has no ego to protect. If he is expert, then he is expert; he feels no need to hide his talents for the sake of false humility. He is, once again, congruent. He is authentic. He does not fear the world seeing him precisely as he is.

Isn't that largely how children behave? They fumble about in their play without regard for looking silly or being judged. They sing and draw and run and dance without any self-image to protect. They play when they need to play. They eat when they need to eat. They rest when they need to rest. And if you ask a child a question, you can be certain they'll do their best to answer it—without any ulterior motive, hidden meaning, or guarded language. "From the mouths of babes" is an expression that honors this truth-telling tendency of young children. This is the organismic trust of children. They've not yet learned to second-guess their feelings or what they have to say. They've not yet learned to feel inadequate for what they don't know or can't do.

Which brings us to the third aspect of full functioning: an *existential orientation*. A life lived from an existential orientation is one that is very much in tune with its unfolding in the here and now. An individual with innate trust in the totality of who she is is freer to live life in the present moment. She doesn't need to selectively edit her experience in order to make it safer and more palatable. She doesn't need to run it through a filter of concepts and defenses in order to make it fit the way it "ought" to. With fewer preconceived notions as to the nature of her self, she is free to become whatever the present moment might "need" her to be.

I doubt I need to convince the reader that children are inherently expert at living in the moment. What is the play of children if not absolute engagement in the moment-to-moment unfolding of the circumstances in which they are immersed? A child can give himself up entirely to his play without concern for how he looks or any perceived need to conform to standards that others have set for him. He isn't pondering for even one instant how any experience will assist him in furthering his play career. He *becomes* his play. And when he's done playing, he will *become* the eating of his snack. Then he will become the taking of his nap.

What would it be like to have such freedom once again? What would it be like to live without our self-imposed constraints? We need only look within. We already know how to see without projecting what we think should be onto everything that comes our way. We already know how to be without measuring every action against those of another. We already know how to engage the world with the fullness and totality of our being rather than with the fragmented and inhibited self that we've become. We only need recall the full functioning of our childhood days.

# Chapter 8: Our Jewel of Wisdom

I hope you've found this to be a worthwhile journey so far. You might be curious, though, as to what you'll take back home with you after finally setting this book aside. Sure, you might be thinking, childhood is a magical and wondrous time for many. But it's not so idyllic for everyone. Besides, we're not children anymore. We're grown up, with bills to pay and problems to solve. How can this recollection of that which we already know be of any benefit to us at this point in our lives? And, anyway, children can be such selfish brats! Isn't the world already buckling under the weight of adult selfishness without our regressing to some idealized childhood state? Fair questions, all of them.

My own childhood was blessed in many regards, with a safe and stable home life and the Nursery in which to blossom forth. I do wonder sometimes what might have been had the long shadow of the Vietnam War not managed to reach me in my wooded paradise. Regardless, that was the nature of the soil in which I took root. The soil from which you sprang may well have included a real war taking place on your neighborhood street or between loved ones behind the walls of your very own home. Each of us has our own unique trials that become all-important to us if for no other reason than their being our own.

Notwithstanding the potentially vast differences in our upbringing, I hope that each of you has at least some recollection of those feelings of belonging, trust, and wonder that I've described—regardless of how brief or infrequent your experience of them may have been. If you can recall even one instant when you enjoyed these feelings, then you can nurture it with the awareness that you presently possess. And those of you whose early childhood memories remain just out of conscious reach, please know that your reality is respected as well. Perhaps your vicarious experiences of the nature of the children in your life at the present time will allow the message contained in these pages to resonate with you all the same.

Regarding the selfishness of children: they *can* be very selfish, despite how limited their self-awareness might be. But I doubt there's any disagreement that children *do* frequently exhibit the qualities discussed throughout this book, qualities that could benefit our broken world if only we would display them more frequently. The key is to marry these finer childlike qualities with the self-awareness of our adult self, thereby facilitating our redemption.

You may be doing this in your spiritual practice already without even realizing what you already know. This is precisely one of the difficulties of being a seeker. Since we don't necessarily have a clear picture of what it is we seek and how we'll know it when we find it, our search can become a never-ending quest. Our heads can become so full of grandiose ideas related to what we think we're going to find that we don't even recognize what we have. We run headlong down this or that path, seeking after God, peace, transcendence, enlightenment, nirvana, or what have you, but we're never really satisfied. We never appreciate what we have. Perhaps it seems too ordinary. Perhaps we think it only exists for those who've reached perfection. Alas, we're just not quite good enough! Remember that?

One of a number of parables contained in the Lotus Sutra, a text held in high regard by many Buddhists, is a story that some refer to as "The Parable of the Jewel in the Robe." The story is referenced on the occasion of five hundred Buddhist saints being assured of their ultimate awakening by the Buddha himself.[10] Up until then, those saints had thought that the best they could hope

---

[10] This sutra purports to be a teaching delivered by the Buddha years after his earthly death. As such, some Buddhists do not give it the same credence as those teachings that were reported to have been heard during his earthly lifetime.

for was the mere cessation of their otherwise endless cycle of death and rebirth into lives of yet more suffering. In this teaching, however, they are assured of nothing less than full Buddhahood.[11] They rejoice in this unexpected, good news, likening their situation to that of a man who falls asleep on the eve of his departure from a wealthy friend. Unbeknownst to him, his wealthy friend sews an expensive jewel into his robe as he sleeps. The friends don't see each other for many years after that, during which time the one with the jewel sewn into his robe experiences numerous travails. When next they meet, the wealthy man can see that his friend has not had an easy life. He calls on him to take note of the jewel in his robe, impressing upon him that he can now use it to never want for anything ever again.

We are like that friend who struggled for so long without realizing what he already possessed. We became intoxicated with our selfhood and forgot the wisdom of our childhood. Even the "saints" in our midst might overlook the forest for the trees, busying themselves with the perfection of rituals and esoteric practices at the risk of reifying selfhood of another ilk. The reality, however, is that we can imbue our existing spiritual practices with deeper meaning and a stronger sense of immediacy by grounding

---

[11] *Anuttara samyak sambodhi*—complete and unsurpassed awakening from which there is no "backsliding."

them in known experience rather than presuming they will take us to some heretofore unknown place.

What then does this "jewel" of childhood wisdom look? If we can recognize its various facets (qualities) in our own experience, then we might use it to guide us back to our full functioning nature. Let's examine these qualities more closely so that we may more readily recognize them when they arise: *wonder*, *belonging*, *trust*, *acceptance*, and *humility*.

What would childhood be without *wonder*? Unfortunately, wonder quickly fades as we grow older. To a child, everything is brand-new and worthy of exploration. As we mature, however, and learn more about the world "around us," we put layer upon layer of conceptualization and explanation between us and the world with which we were once so seamlessly integrated. How did the world begin? Some say God created it. Others are certain that it started with the big bang. Still others think it might be both or maybe something else entirely. Regardless, as soon as we think we know the answer, our wonder becomes diminished. One explanation at a time, our wonder becomes diminished. We separate from the world. And as that separation grows, the world comes to be seen for its utility rather than as the very ground of our being.

Perhaps the child who once wondered grows up to be a scientist who makes a living trying to understand and explain— certainly a noble occupation. And yet there is a risk, or even a likelihood, that her wonder will become co-opted by a desire for monetary gain or enhanced status within the scientific community. Wonder may morph into the urge to understand the world so that it might be brought under control. The pure wonder of her childhood years will then have become supplanted by the more utilitarian exploration that takes place in research and development laboratories of corporations all over the world.

Of course, there are worse fates than this. We can become so far removed from wonder that we grow world-weary and jaded. We might think we have the world all figured out, like some game that we've played so many times that the only thing standing between us and hopeless boredom is the uncertainty of the next roll of the dice or turn of the card. We can become so insulated within our world of ideas that the real world remains forever outside of our experience, never to be wondered at again.

On the other hand, we might fancy ourselves filled with wonder—gobbling up worldly facts as if we're eating popcorn at a blockbuster movie, drinking in scientific discovery as if we're gulping down an ice-cold soft drink. Unfortunately, such shallow wonder has more to do with the enhancement of the self than its transcendence. The self wants more and more. It can never get enough, know enough, be enough, or experience enough. Wonder of this sort amounts to little more than entertainment that keeps us from joining the ranks of the world-weary and jaded.

Unlike its faded replacements, the wonder of children is a question that we rejoice in without any expectation of ever receiving an answer. It's a bright, plump, juicy piece of fruit that we behold without the desire to consume it ever entering our mind. Desire, after all, requires both subject and object, but the wonder of children is the very transcendence of subject and object. More precisely, the wonder of children precedes the creation of those bite-sized pieces of the world that become so amenable to our consumption.

How then are we adults to nurture in the here and now the wonder of our childhood years? We can begin by making time to be still and watch what goes on around us and within us, without any desire to learn or see or feel anything in particular. We don't need to do anything other than remain open to whatever arises. No matter where we are, we can be like that child that we once were, sitting still beside the pond of existence, listening and watching. Call it prayer, meditation, or communion with nature. Call it taking time out to simply be. Remember, though, the child that you once were wouldn't have felt the need to call it anything at all!

Find a patch of grass somewhere. Sit still and pass the time— or create it, if you will. It may seem like nothing but a patch of grass at first, but over time it will reveal itself to be so much more. Maybe you'll find that you're actually sitting on a variety of grasses, clover, plantain, and weeds. You needn't try to name them though.

Simply notice them for what they are. Are there any critters crawling in the shadows between the earth and the stalks and leaves? Open up to their presence. Let your fingers find the earth from which all those various plants and critters (and you) arise. Does it feel cool? Moist? Dry? Simply notice the sensations. There's no need for analysis. Likewise, your thoughts. When they visit you, simply notice them and let them go. Allow time to settle into everything that's going on around you and within.

Lay back and look up at the sky if you so choose. Do you notice any gradations of color? Do you see whatever spots and squiggles might exist in your perfectly imperfect field of vision? Feel the earth against your back. Settle into the support that it provides. Do you feel your heart beating? Do you notice your breath coming and going, keeping you alive from moment to moment? These things are not the essentials of some recipe however. Consider their mention merely an invitation to open up to your unique experience of being alive. Forget all your expectations for what the moment "should" be, especially the nagging notion that you should be doing something else. Forget that you're doing anything at all. Nowhere else has the universe given rise to precisely what exists within you and around you at this moment. Nothing stands between you and the farthest reaches of space and time. Get close enough to this miracle, and wonder will arise—wordless, transcendent wonder.

While a natural place can be especially conducive to wonder, you can actually find it anywhere. You can even find it in an industrial environment by closing your eyes and listening to the sounds. The rumbling and whirring, hissing and clunking will begin to wash over you and through you. But don't try to label the sounds or determine their origins. Don't try to ascertain whether the materials involved are stone or steel, rubber or wood. Simply listen. Hear them without resorting to words. Feel them in your body. Allow them to become you. How else can sound exist but with your body, ears, and mind? You already know how to "see" in this way. Just make a little space and time in your life to actually do it.

To wonder we can add *belonging*, a quality that I'll introduce with a brief story. While backpacking in the mountains, it sometimes occurs to me that I'm like an astronaut visiting another planet. I have enough food and water and appropriate gear to protect me from the elements. But my meager life support system will only last a short time. All too soon I'll need to go back to where I "belong." Sure, if I were a better outdoorsman, I might extend my visit by an appreciable length of time. But even the best outdoorsman must make his way back to civilization eventually. It's a rare individual indeed who can head off into the forest to live indefinitely, as if she belongs there.

On the other hand, the plants and animals of the natural world always belong. Their very existence is proof of this. A seed sprouts because conditions were right for it. It belongs. An animal is born because its parents found food and shelter enough to bring it into this world. It, too, belongs. We modern humans, however, have a conflicted relationship with the natural world. We don't just put down roots and reach toward the sun. We don't just forage for food and burrow for shelter wherever we might find ourselves. We have more precise and complicated requirements than these, endlessly precise and complicated it sometimes seems. Whereas wild things always belong, we humans struggle to belong even in those places that are totally designed to meet our needs—our cities. We've grown too distant from the natural world in order to feel that we belong there, and yet our man-made world too often fosters in us loneliness and alienation instead of the belongingness that we crave.

Our struggle commences as our burgeoning individuality begins to nudge us from the cozy nest of belongingness that is our family home—the place where we acquired the emotional template for what we'll be searching for out in the larger world. And even if our family home was not as supportive as it could have been, we still likely acquired some sense of what we missed, what our family life "should" have been like. Regardless, each of us eventually heads off to school alone where we struggle to fit into at least one of the various groups or cliques that inevitably form there. We struggle to become educated in order to fit into this complex and unforgiving modern economy. We struggle to get our foot in the door of some company so that we can work our way up the career ladder to the place where we think we'll belong. We struggle to fit in with our neighbors, coworkers, and fellow spiritual travelers. We struggle to find a partner with whom we can belong in the most intimate sense so that we might create a cozy nest of our own in which to belong for the remainder of our days.

All our lives we struggle to belong, and every now and again we taste its sweetness. But then we get laid off or our work ceases to be as fulfilling as it once was. Our friends move on. Our social networks dissolve. Our relationship with our partner comes to an end. Perhaps our relationship with our spiritual community begins to sour or become tired. And then our struggle begins all over again to carve out a place in this wilderness of modernity where we might feel that sense of belonging all over again.

But might there be a place where we always belong, no matter what has happened to us or who we have become? I'm not thinking of any physical place where we might find ourselves. I'm thinking of a state of mind, a realization of who and what and where we really are. Forget everything about yourself that might exist in some file or database regarding your financial assets, credentials, or qualifications. Such measures amount to nothing in the grand scheme of things. Forget everything about where you think you came from or where you think you're going. Those are mere distractions from this moment here and now. Forget your name. Forget your face. Nothing that is really meaningful has anything to do with either one. In the vastness of the space-time of our universe, you are an observing consciousness born of unique causes and conditions that will never be repeated. Like the wild animals born of their parents, and the windblown seeds that find a spot of earth in which to root, you belong. You are the universe observing the universe. You belong.

Such truth went without saying when we were younger and without complicated ideas as to who and what we are. We needed no coaching then in order to dedicate our entire being to observation and wonder. We belonged without even trying to belong. Unfortunately, the stronger our sense of self becomes, the more focused we become on where our edges meet the world. The stronger our sense of self becomes, the more easily we overlook the fact that we arise from the world as opposed to being born into it. In other words, the more complicated we become, the more difficult it is for us to feel that we belong. So much must be just so.

What is the belongingness of your experience? Is it a childhood memory of warmth, caring, and protection? Do you feel it amongst your friends, your kin, or your spiritual companions? Is yours the belongingness of Christianity—that of the prostitutes and tax collectors, the centurions and criminals, and all the otherwise unwelcome people who belong just as much as everyone else belongs within the Kingdom of God? Is it the belongingness of Buddhism, in which everything is dependent upon everything else for its very existence? How can anything *not* belong when everything is dependent on everything else? Is it the belongingness of Hinduism, of Brahman manifested as all things? How can anything *not* belong when everything is already that which is most divine?

There are many ways to think of it and many ways to experience it. But if you need a hint as to how to get in touch with belongingness in the deepest and most inalienable sense, try finding that place on the grass once again. Lay back and gaze up at the sky. Forget what you've become or whatever it is you think you've done with your life. Become the child that you once were, without a past and without a future. The universe has given rise to you. You are the universe perceiving itself. Nothing else is expected of you. This is your birthright. This is where you belong. Ah, but can you trust that it is so?

*Trust* can be difficult to maintain in a world where little remains the same for long. Family and friends pass away. Belief and meaning slip all too easily from our grasp. Things that we enjoy are taken from us or cease to be as pleasurable as they once were. Yes, we are inextricably part of this ever-changing world and, frequently enough, we are the ones that end up changing long before what we used to love has either changed or ceased to be. Thus, some of us learn to trust only in our ability to always get what we want. Sure, we and the world are always changing. The one constant, though, or so it might seem, is our ability to go out and get what we want, no matter what the changing circumstances might be. Thus, we find solace only in our own resilience and adaptability. Look closely though. What is the real nature of the currency that we possess? If it's not money, then perhaps it's our network of connections, our looks, or our charm. Perhaps it's our intelligence or shrewdness, our intimidating presence or physical prowess. We might find it difficult to envision this "currency" ever being taken from us, but change itself has a way of taking from us everything that we hold dear.

What then can we trust in to never ever change? What in this world is true and constant? Where is our rock amid so much shifting sand? Religion is that rock for many, of course. But trust in God, or whatever description of metaphysical reality one's chosen religion might espouse, is difficult to maintain for an entire lifetime. While religion might provide a strong foundation for many a meaningful year, even the strongest of foundations can be collapsed by the quake of waning faith. How many times have we heard someone wonder what kind of God would stand by and let such a thing happen whenever a child is brutally slain or taken by disease before experiencing all that life can be? Indeed, belief in a God that will forever protect us and our loved ones on account of our faith and devotion is just one tragedy away from crumbling. But faith can wane even without such an occurrence. Simply "living into" a belief system can reveal areas where we must stretch and strain too much in order to make it fit. Thus, even one's self-proclaimed rock of faith is not immune to the winds of change.

For the winds of change include the changing hearts and minds of every one of us.

How then can we ever really trust; and what do we place our trust in when we do? The answer lies in that which we already know—the trust in being itself that every child has. This innate trust can either be nurtured or neglected depending upon the circumstances in which the child is raised. But even if it is roundly trampled, it is never completely destroyed.

The trust of children is such that everything is taken at face value. A child has no need for the reassurance of his parents prior to being exposed to the darker realities of the world. If he's not yet heard of or experienced tragedy in any way, then the thought of it can gain no purchase in his mind. But once tragedy does find its way into his imaginings, once he does become in need of reassurance, he has no reason to doubt when his parents tell him that "nothing bad like that could ever happen to you," or "of course, we'll always be here to take care of you." How can a child possibly doubt a parent's word if he's never been given any reason to doubt their word before? A child's trust is not based upon belief. A child's trust is not based upon imaginings and supposition. It is based entirely on his experience of being, nothing more.

But how can such an observation about the trust of children help those of us who are long in years and saddled with a wealth of accumulated experiences that give us no recourse *but* to doubt? How can we ever learn to trust in any way that even remotely resembles the innocent trust of children? One way is to dispense with belief altogether. Without belief, there is no faith that can be shaken. Without belief, we can only see things as they are. Without belief, we learn to trust that which we see. Of course, readers with a belief in God might be shocked by such a suggestion. Please bear with me though. Is it possible for you to *experience* God as opposed to merely *believing* in him or her? If so, how? The attentive reader will have already picked up on the fact that I have a few thoughts in that regard.

Which brings us to the final two of the five facets of the jewel of wisdom that I'll be exploring here: *acceptance* and *humility*. The two are so closely related that it hardly seems possible to consider one without the other. How often do we declare something unacceptable because it doesn't measure up to what we think we deserve instead? These accommodations might be acceptable to a vagabond, for instance, but not for someone of our standing. This meal might be acceptable to one with far less refined taste but not to us. That tone of voice might be acceptable when speaking to just anyone off the street, but we're not just anyone off the street, are we?

I spoke earlier of how the stronger our sense of self becomes, the more focused we become on where our edges meet the world. These are good examples of the potential for conflict between the reality of how the world is treating us and our ideas regarding how the world should be treating us for our self-image to be upheld. A person with humility to spare can much more readily accept those unpleasant situations that might chafe one who is otherwise challenged in this regard.

Lackluster dinners, substandard lodging, and rude exchanges are inconsequential in the grand scheme of things. Frequently enough, though, things happen that completely and permanently derail whatever plans we might have had or sense of normalcy we might have felt. Severe illness or accident, broken relationships, career setbacks, financial devastation, the death of a loved one— none of these are easy to accept. At first blush, it may not seem that humility has anything at all to do with our acceptance of these more tragic twists and turns in life, but it does. Haven't we all wondered at least once why something was happening to us, as if we were somehow too precious for the universe to mistreat? Stars can explode, earthquakes and hurricanes can devastate entire cities, acts of genocide can annihilate millions of people, but somehow the universe should tread gently around us due to the inherent specialness of our being! Indeed, there is little humility in such thinking, but let us also be quick to forgive the irrationality of our own grieving self.

Children, on the other hand, are masters of acceptance. It might not seem that way if you've witnessed a temper tantrum recently, but consider for a moment how children weather a serious accident, illness, or hardship. No, they're not immune to pain, but they *are* immune to much of the suffering that befalls an adult with the same prognosis. The reason for this is that a child's awareness resides much more frequently in the present moment than does the awareness of an adult. Both the child and the adult are aware of their pain in the here and now. The adult, however, is much more likely to suffer from the mental anguish that frequently accompanies the experience of pain.

Adults are much more likely to be dwelling in the past or living in the future. We pine for the way things were before the accident, illness, or hardship befell us. We ruminate over what we might have done in order to have avoided the pain of the present. Perhaps we ponder how life will be shorter now, without the abilities that we once took for granted and with much less meaning and enjoyment. Perhaps we become angry with our God for letting bad things happen to us despite our great faith. Perhaps we become angry with all those who seem to enjoy much better circumstances than we do, despite being so much less deserving than we are. And why does the world have to be this way anyway? Why are our bodies so fragile? Why is it so hard to find happiness? Yes, leave it to the vicissitudes of life to reveal all the many ways our lack of humility can show its true colors.

Another reason that children are more accepting than adults is that they are much less likely to harbor illusions as to what they *should* be able to do. We adults have so many more expectations for ourselves than we're even aware of. We *should* be able to beat whatever illness we might contract. We *should* be able to recover from whatever accident might befall us. We *should* be able to overcome every difficulty with some ingenious and life-improving solution. We *should* be able to acquire all the trappings of our modern, materialistic society. We *should* be able to find work to support ourselves and our families, even though the economy has grown so out of sync with the needs of so many. Children are not caught up in such a tangle of ideas. They're children, after all, and almost everything they encounter is bigger and stronger than they are! Children have no expectation that they should be in control of whatever situation they might be facing. And we all know what thrives in the empty space between what is and what *should* be: depression, anxiety, and meaninglessness.

Humility is an underappreciated trait in our culture. We celebrate those with the utmost refinement of taste and those who speak with the greatest audacity and self-assurance. We celebrate the winners who go after what they want and who then let everyone else know that they've prevailed. I suppose when we celebrate such traits in the kings and queens of politics, sports, industry, and popular culture, we celebrate them in ourselves as well. Perhaps we need assurance that this self of ours really is worth all the time and energy that we invest in its creation and perpetuation.

I've focused in this chapter on those spiritual attributes that children innately possess but which tend to become attenuated or obscured as we grow older. Ironically, it's often only after we've fully matured and begun to struggle with our "grown-up" lives that we come to sense that something is missing. We're just not quite sure what. Perhaps experiences of loss or alienation prompt us to embrace or reengage in religious exploration in the hopes of finding what we don't yet realize we once enjoyed without any effort whatsoever. So, we struggle some more. And perhaps we grow more jaded, disillusioned, or unfulfilled along the way. It can be hard to find what we're looking for when we're not even sure what it is!

My hope is that readers will look closer to home before assuming that the answer lies on the other side of some intricate practice or presently incomprehensible teaching. At their core, the various religions exist to guide us to something that inherently resides within us. Unfortunately, even those in positions of religious power do not necessarily act as if this is true. All too often they become so intoxicated with the "specialness" of their position in some hierarchical structure that they lose track of the specialness of everyone else.

Religion stems from the deepest and most universal longing that humans share. It is rooted in the very neurobiology by which we experience the world. Whatever ineffable religious visions, ecstatic states, transcendental experiences, or sensations of communion with God we might enjoy arise from this neurobiological structure that we all share. It's only after we try to put these ineffable experiences into words or position them within some presumed metaphysical framework that the various religions of the world become recognizable.

Most religious adherents swim only on the surface of their respective traditions, where the "waves" may appear to be very different than those of any other religion. They rarely dive into the depths. The depths are where the waters become still. There, without the distractions of crashing waves, the ineffable is more readily experienced. Sadly, the same can be said of many religious leaders. Like good ship captains, they dutifully steer their charges through calm and stormy seas alike, without being able to guide them to the depths of universal stillness.

That which is universal is present in us from the earliest age. These explorations of wonder, belonging, trust, acceptance, and humility are meant to facilitate our reengagement with the universal depths that we used to know so well. Perhaps what I've written here will serve to deepen and strengthen your experience of whatever religious tradition you might call home. On the other hand, it might also serve to bolster your belief that all religious experience is merely a mythic interpretation of biologically explainable phenomena. I'm not in control of what you do with that which you already know. I intend only to bring it into sharper focus.

Wonder has never left us. The potential for the wide-eyed, direct experience of reality that was so common in our childhood is still within us somewhere. It's merely been covered over with explanation and conceptualization. Now, there's nothing inherently wrong with explanation and conceptualization as long as we don't let it get in the way of our direct experience of reality. For it is our ability to experience reality most directly that is our wisdom.

Belonging is still with us as well. That sense of safety, connection, and even oneness that we (hopefully) experienced in our families and in our earliest experiences of the natural world is still with us, if only as something that we long to re-experience. We used to trust in our belonging so completely that we were fearlessly free to be whatever it was that our being was blossoming into in any given moment. Unfortunately, though, we got sidetracked along the way with concerns that are meaningless in the ultimate sense.

The acceptance of that which is comes much more naturally to children. Our realization of the futility of our ongoing struggles with the ever-changing circumstances of our existence is a return to the wisdom that we once embodied. Before we came to believe in, crave, and celebrate our ability to control every aspect of our lives, we embodied the humility to know that we could not. This, too, is the innate wisdom with which we are born.

It's one thing to recognize these various spiritual attributes as being integral to our childhood being. It's quite another to recognize their place in our adult lives. And it's another thing altogether to work toward making them an integral part of everyday life once we've lost touch with them along the way. Shall we count on our recognition of their meaningfulness to somehow precipitate their regular appearance in our day-to-day lives? Shall we hope that our insight into their importance will, in and of itself, nurture their actualization? This will be the topic of the next and final chapter of this book.

# Chapter 9: Mind, Body, World

It likely goes without saying that I was a quiet child, pulled as if by some magnetic attraction to places of solitude that weren't always easy to find. You see, my father was then a young schoolteacher, with a family that was fast outgrowing our modest home. Compounding matters was the fact that entrance to my older sister's bedroom required passage straight through mine. Thus, I had no quiet space inside that I could really call my own. I had to find it.

And that is how the Nursery became my refuge from the moment I was old enough to venture out beyond the garden gate. I could be alone there to enjoy the silence whenever I needed. Perhaps that's another reason Mark Patrick's tiny room was so appealing, sparse as a monk's quarters though it was. Sure, his half brother was around for at least some of the time, but things must be different with a brother, I likely reasoned.

But this is not to say that I never had the opportunity to enjoy a little silence inside our home. Notwithstanding the tight quarters, I still managed from time to time to find a way to be alone. One such place of occasional refuge was in my parents' bedroom during the day. No, we weren't allowed to play there, but enjoying silence wasn't play as far as I was concerned. Thus, I must have felt that I was within bounds whenever I slipped inside for the sole purpose of being alone.

My parents kept a clock radio on the shelf of their headboard. It was a 1950s model that they'd received as a wedding gift, with a pink plastic case that had ridges molded into it around the clock face and over the adjacent speaker. I'd lie on the bed facing it, with my elbows on the pillows and my chin resting on my forearms. I liked to run my fingernail across the plastic ridges covering the speaker. It sounded like a tiny plastic xylophone due to the varying lengths of the ridges over the circular opening.

Most of all, though, I liked to listen to the drone of the clock motor as the second hand traced out minute after minute after minute. It hummed steadily as the second hand fell past the one and the two, down toward the six. Errrrrrrrrrr … However, once the motor began lifting it from the six to the seven, it had to work a little harder. Err, rerr, rerr, rerr … With my eyes closed, I experienced the minutes as having a rhythm to them. The motor lifted the second hand and let it fall back down again. One minute. It lifted the hand and let it fall back down again. Two minutes. Err, rerr, rerr, rerr ..., errrrrrrrrr ... Three minutes. Err, rerr, rerr, rerr ..., errrrrrrrrr ... Four minutes. The motor lifted the hand and let it fall back down again. Five minutes.

I became fascinated with the workings of my body and the passage of time. My heartbeats came too quickly for me to measure, like the seconds slipping past, but my breath was much more easily quantified. It took thus and such time to go from inhalation to exhalation and back again. The longer I lay there, though, the deeper I settled into stillness and the more drawn out my breathing became. It was only natural that I eventually took to seeing how long I could hold my breath.

Now, anyone who tries to see how long they can hold their breath quickly realizes how it's done. You breathe deeply and quickly for several breaths, culminating with one last big inhalation right before you commence. Something happens, though, as soon as you actually begin to hold your breath. Your awareness recedes from the outside world and begins to focus on the inner workings of the body. The beating of your heart slows. Your thoughts, too, begin to slow. You become aware of every gurgle in your belly and ringing in your ears. You notice the changing colors and flashes of light that play across your field of closed-eyed "vision."

Like a stone sinking to the bottom of a lake, I went down, down, down ..., there to settle on the bottom, immersed in glorious stillness. Err, rerr, rerr, rerr ..., errrrrrrrrr ... The motor lifted the second hand and let it fall back down again. It strained and then relaxed. My heart pounded in my ears. It did its double thump, and then it relaxed. It double-thumped, and then it relaxed. My mind became the motor lifting the second hand and letting it fall back down again. My mind became my pounding heart, slow and solid. Ba-boom …, ba-boom …, ba-boom … And then, amid that deep and steady pounding, my mind became still—utterly and profoundly still.

It didn't take much longer, though, for my mind to become the increasingly insistent urge to take another breath. First, it became the sensation of wanting to take a breath. Then, it became the sensation of needing to take a breath. Thereafter, it became the sensation of the effort required to refrain from taking a breath. Finally, it became that next breath—glorious, expansive, fresh, life-giving, rejuvenating.

Perhaps such recollections of spontaneous childhood meditations allowed me to quickly grasp the Zen teaching that body and mind are not two. They're so inextricably linked as to make it impossible to speak deeply of one without consideration of the other. Thus, when I first learned that we become enlightened with the body, not with the mind, it made perfect sense to me. It corresponded with what I'd already experienced as a child—before letting it fall by the wayside forgotten, that is.

We all forget, it seems. By the time we reach adulthood, it's all but second nature to think of body and mind as separate and distinct. Even one who is very much in tune with his body might think of it more as a beast of burden to be trained by the mind or a tool to be skillfully used by it. Leave it to children and Zen masters, and perhaps a very few others, to really understand the inextricable oneness of body and mind.

But why is this such an important point? Three reasons come to mind. First, it helps us understand how we fit into the world. More precisely, it helps us understand that we don't *fit* into the world at all. We arise in it and from it. The earth gives rise to this body. Our body, in turn, supports our brain and the mental processes with which we so closely identify—our mind. We are a blossoming forth from the ground of being, whether we believe this ground to have been created by God, to indeed *be* God, or to simply consist of the "stuff" of which the universe is made. Thus, we belong, and we can trust in this belonging as the most fundamental reality of life. We might choose to believe more than this, but to believe other than this is simply not in keeping with the fundamental nature of reality.

In other words, we're not some self-existent entity deposited here from somewhere else. Sure, we might be tempted to think otherwise, given the separateness that we so often feel or the completeness with which we identify with whatever thoughts are going on inside our head. But thoughts are merely one aspect of consciousness; and consciousness is wholly dependent upon the structure of the brain, the body in which the brain resides, and the fact that the body is always in contact with the "outside" world.

Every thought that can possibly arise does so from the reality that is "out there." All the visions, imaginings, ponderings, and musings that the mind is capable of producing are based on what it has thus far experienced. We might say then that the activity of the mind is entirely derivative. Notwithstanding its awesome creative potential, the mind cannot conjure up something out of nothing.

A second reason that understanding the seamless integration of body and mind is so important is that it helps us root our spiritual practice in the rich soil of experience rather than in the barrenness of ideas and conceptualization. In this way, our practice becomes more than just an intellectual endeavor. It becomes an outgrowth of reality itself, arising with the body, which arises from the ground of being.

Regardless of where we think we came from or where we think we're going, we're always here in this present moment, continuously arising from and along with all other phenomena. It seems compelling then, regardless of our spiritual orientation, that we strive to bring the insights of our practice to bear on the circumstances of this present moment and everything with which we arise.[12] In other words, no matter what our metaphysical beliefs might be, no matter what we might believe about the existence or nature of God, no matter what we might believe about souls or the

_____

[12] The reality that all phenomena arise along with and as a result of other phenomena is referred to by Buddhists as *dependent origination*.

afterlife, the reality of our arising from a shared ground of existence compels us to bring the highest values of our spirituality to bear in our everyday lives, for the sake of everyone and everything.

Finally, an accurate understanding of the seamless nature of body and mind allows us to fully realize what it means to become "enlightened with the body." Now, there are many *ideas* floating around about the nature of enlightenment. When I use the term, however, I'm simply referring to an awareness of things precisely as they are, without our seeing them through a lens of some presumed, desired, or conditioned interpretation. Enlightened awareness is a matter of letting go of the various and sundry ideas we've come to hold dear over the course of our fall—ideas that hinder us from seeing things precisely as they are. But what does the body have to do with letting go of the ideas that we hold dear? What does the body have to do with us seeing things as they are?

Becoming enlightened with the body might make more sense if we simply remember that which we already know. For instance, when I was a young child visiting those beloved frog ponds out in the Nursery, I became profoundly aware that my presence changed everything. Upon my arrival, everything that could scurry or fly away from my abrupt intrusion did so and everything that could duck deeper into the shadowed waters or hide amongst the weed stems did so as well. Upon my becoming still, however, I began to see things as they really were. Mosquito larvae would begin to squiggle back up to the sun-warmed surface of the pond. Water striders would begin again their back-and-forth maneuvering. Frogs would reappear and begin to sing as so few people are ever allowed to witness. And the dragonflies and birds would return from wary vigil on the outskirts such that their nature became known. I learned then that it wasn't merely my presence that made the difference, it was the *nature* of my presence that made the difference. As a noisy intruder, I was banished from the kingdom. As one filled with a will to do and control, I was forbidden to witness things as they were. When I was still, however, all things began to manifest their true nature for me to see.

Zen adepts often compare the enlightened mind to a perfect mirror reflecting the entire world without adding to it or subtracting from it, without distorting it in any way whatsoever. In order to be so, however, the mind must be still. But stilling the mind is difficult when one does not yet understand the inseparable nature of body and mind. It might seem that stilling the mind requires learning some mental technique in order that we might turn off our mental activity as we turn off a television set. On the contrary, the most direct route to stilling the mind is via stilling the body. Think of a bowl of water. When the bowl is jostled about, the surface of the water remains disturbed. When the bowl is left to become still, however, the surface of the water eventually becomes like a mirror—reflecting the world around it.

After abiding in stillness for a time, our mind naturally begins to grow calm. When we're sitting with our hands in our lap or resting on our thighs, relatively little tactile stimulation remains to be processed. Our kinesthetic and proprioceptive senses, likewise, are given a break from the usually much more complex task of keeping track of our body's movement and positioning in space and time. Furthermore, if our eyes are closed or nearly so, then our very robust visual processing capacity is left with relatively little to do. As such, abiding in stillness is a little like floating in a sensory deprivation tank, although not quite so extreme. Both experiences involve a withdrawal from sensory stimulation, and both experiences affect the activity of the conscious mind.

But just as being in a sensory deprivation tank can be disorienting to the point of prompting hallucinations, so the stillness of meditation or contemplation can occasionally bring forth false apparitions and sensations. The brain, unused to the scarcity of stimulation, continues its usual level of activity by finding new things on which to focus or by perceiving things that don't really exist at all—like when we strain to see something in the fading twilight and end up imagining all sorts of things that aren't really there.[13] With time, however, the brain grows accustomed to the stillness of meditation or contemplation, and the potential for such experiences subsides. The brain's conditioned need to fill the newfound mental spaciousness with

---

[13] *Makyo* is the Japanese term for such apparitions, some of which might tempt the meditation practitioner to believe that he or she has acquired some special capability.

unnecessary thoughts and perceptions begins to subside, and the mind begins to experience ever deeper levels of stillness. It becomes more mirror-like, neither adding to nor subtracting from the experience of that which is. In a manner of speaking, we can say that virtually all aspects of our karma—those created patterns that prompt us to behave in certain ways and interpret the world around us in certain ways—have ceased to hold sway over us. Our reactivity to various stimuli subsides, and the passions of our conditioned existence become stilled.

In this light, let's revisit that excerpt from the *Xinxin Ming* that I presented earlier:

> *The nature of reality is unobscured*
> *As long as one refrains from making judgments.*
> *Begin to make distinctions, however,*
> *And heaven becomes cleaved from earth.*

Our conditioned ways of thinking and feeling lead us to make judgments and distinctions regarding right and wrong, good and bad, ugly and beautiful, self and other. Unfortunately, true seeing is curtailed as soon as judgment is asserted. While we're engaged in meditation or silent contemplation, however, these conditioned ways of thinking and feeling exist more or less in abeyance. Our mind can become so still that it sees things only as they are. For a time, heaven and earth are seen again as one. For a time, the kingdom of God is at hand. For a time, we experience the *suchness* that was so much more common in our childhood years, when the world was fresh and bright and new and our sense of self was not so strong.

Ah, but time passes. Eventually we rise again from stillness and proceed to live out our ordinary lives. Our conditioning takes hold of us once again and our experience of suchness, oneness, or grace begins to fade. Fortunately, though, the strength of our conditioning becomes diminished for our having once again become familiar with stillness of mind. We begin to more clearly see our thought processes, just as we more clearly see the world around us. Perhaps all we can do at first is notice them, but with continued practice, these created patterns of seeing and interpreting our experiences further dissolve, thereby ceasing to control us. As such, the judgments and distinctions we might make in our day-to-day lives become informed with greater wisdom and deeper compassion for our having seen things just a little more clearly than we otherwise would have seen them.

Whatever we might call our experience of stillness—be it meditation, silent contemplation, wordless prayer, or simply abiding—little conceptualization is required for the practitioner to recognize its importance. We simply must taste it once again. Different traditions conceptualize and contextualize it in different ways. Once we look beyond the associated metaphysical constructs, however, we can see the underlying commonality.

For instance, you've probably heard the Sanskrit word *nirvana* used in reference to some heavenly state of blissful transcendence that only the most dedicated Buddhists or Hindu yogis may come to enjoy. Figurative definitions of the word generally encompass some form of emancipation from this earthly existence—liberation from the worldly passions that keep us trapped in a cycle of death and rebirth. Literal definitions suggest images of a fire having been extinguished or firewood having been used up. The fire being extinguished, of course, is the very karma that brings our being into existence. The way to extinguish it is to become calm, quiet, and immovable. Thus, a practice that a Zen adept might describe as allowing him or her to wake up and clearly see in the here and now might be described by a Hindu yogi as providing the means to bring an end to the cycle of death and rebirth for the sake of eternal union with the divine.

Many Christian traditions, likewise, hold the experience of stillness in high regard. Central to an unprogrammed Quaker religious service, for instance, is the communal practice of settling into silence in order for "that of God" to become known. On the other hand, a Christian contemplative from the Catholic tradition might begin with a scriptural reading, gradually transition into a period of reflection and discursive prayer, and then ultimately settle into silent contemplation. This experience of stillness is referred to by some as "coming to rest in God."

Unfortunately, such contemplative prayer became increasingly intellectualized and marginalized over the course of the last half millennium. It even came to be viewed by some as a potentially dangerous endeavor.[14] The possibility that the sensory-deprived contemplative might experience one of those aforementioned hallucinatory apparitions was deemed tantamount to opening oneself up to demonic influence, an interesting interpretation given that the Japanese term for such meditative experiences, *makyo*, translates loosely as "devil's realm."

It comes as no surprise to me that there would be such commonality of religious or spiritual experience as has been noted here regarding stillness and silence. We humans share the same basic physiology, after all. This is so with respect to our bodies as well as our brains. Except for a few idiosyncratic differences, our neurobiological structure is the same. We all live and breathe and think as human beings. We all have the capacity to experience stillness as human beings. However, while this experience of stillness might be the same in a qualitative way, any individual's subsequent description of it may vary greatly depending upon his or her intellectual development, vocabulary, life experience, worldview, and belief system. Whereas one might think he's caught a glimpse of Buddha mind, another might believe she's progressing

---

[14] Father Thomas Keating provides a nice summary of this history in *Open Mind, Open Heart.*

toward ultimate liberation, and yet another might say he's been resting in the presence of God. How could it be any other way when people speak of something that is largely ineffable?

But let's not be tempted to dismiss the importance of stillness simply because so many different and seemingly contradictory words have been written about it. In keeping with what I stated earlier with respect to belonging: we might choose to believe more than is present regarding the metaphysical context in which we experience stillness, but to believe other than what is present—to deny the experience itself—is simply not in keeping with the fundamental nature of reality.

Where there is meaningful religious practice, there is stillness. And where there is stillness, there is the potential for transformational human experience. Life on earth will be transformed if we simply return to a more childlike state imbued with wonder, belonging, trust, acceptance, and humility. No, I'm not advocating that we become more childish. If anything, modern adulthood is marked by some of the worst examples of childishness writ large: self-absorption, the inability to see things from the point of view of another, the lack of a social and long-term perspective, the need for instant gratification, the potential for violent anger. But if we have no problem accepting and even celebrating such childish traits as these, why would we disparage the cultivation of those positive traits that will be of benefit in returning us to wholeness—as individuals, as community, and as a species living in harmony with an ecologically rich and healthy earth? It's not all that mysterious. It's that which we already know.

# Epilogue

The back gate of the very first home I ever knew opened onto a tract of land that I'll not forget for as long as I may live. That was how this book began, and it's a fitting end for it as well. For even though that land has long since been paved over, it still exists in wondrous glory within my mind. I simply need swing open the gate and stroll on through. And if it should come to pass—many years from now I hope—that I enjoy a peaceful end to this mysterious existence that is "my" life, then I'll unlatch that gate once more to walk out into the suchness of the Nursery one last time, there to sit beside one of those frog ponds as consciousness gradually slips away.

I say this not with any treacly sense of nostalgia or melodramatic flair. Rather, I say it with deep gratitude for my having experienced in that place something akin to the proverbial Garden of Eden before the fall. I say it with gratitude for my having been given the opportunity, albeit after a long and sometimes difficult search, to realize the significance of all that I learned there long ago. Most of all, though, I say it with deep conviction that the most important lesson I ever learned in this life was revealed to me in that place: that stillness is the pond beside which we long to sit; stillness is the home to which we long to return.

In myriad ways, via numerous paths, we're all trying to find our way back home. The difficulty is that the landmarks we might use to orient ourselves are all too easily overlooked. The loud voices of the fallen keep us distracted. The endeavors of the lost seem so much more enticing than anything going on in our "ordinary" lives. Nevertheless, stillness awaits. We simply need look within. Our natural experiences of wonder, belonging, trust, acceptance, and humility will not lead us astray.

It's difficult to live in a world that has fallen and is falling still. It's difficult to sit still while everyone around us races down the road to anywhere other than where they are. Yes, and all too often I find myself racing down that road along with everybody else, with the added sadness of knowing exactly what I'm doing. For I'm reminded of my fall every time I catch a glimpse of one of those still wild places down in an overgrown culvert alongside the highway or on one of those odd parcels of land too small or inaccessible to be of any appreciable commercial value.

The saddest part of all, though, is that it's becoming harder and harder to find places such as the Nursery, places that can nurture in us that which we already know, thereby allowing us to find our way back home. Like tiny islands inundated by a rising tide, those still wild places are becoming submerged by an ever-rising ocean of modernity. I was fortunate to have been something of a country boy growing up on the fringe of expanding suburbia. But what of the children growing up today with entertainment center playpens, manicured backyards, and manufactured playgrounds? What will happen when all those still wild places have disappeared, and no one remains who can even remember them? Could that which we already know one day become that which is lost forever?

I know just a little bit of what it must be like to be lost forever. For some years, I worked at a corporate job that kept me mentally and physically confined for most of my waking hours and preoccupied for much of the rest. I was probably never more out of touch with who and what I am than during that time. I yearned to simply be, but I was strangely unsure of what that meant. Nonetheless, there was something deep inside of me that was guiding me back home. For it was then that I began to realize what those still wild places were telling me.

It came to me like a vision: that ride through the Nursery on my bicycle in near darkness, with the honey locust council keenly watching my every move. I remembered how the trees and underbrush and rocks and grass seemed to reach out to me from

147

darkness as I passed. They were reaching out to me once again. But whereas in my childhood they evoked in me some of my first tremblings of fearful self-awareness, in adulthood they represented nothing less than my salvation. They were reaching out to me from the light this time. Those still wild places represented my deepest yearning to be free.

I quit that corporate job for the sake of a livelihood more in keeping with my newfound understanding of what life is all about. I also began anew and in earnest my exploration of the "spiritual realm"—rooting more deeply in actual practice that which had been a much more intellectual pursuit. But it wasn't until I'd made the connection between these various landmarks I've been speaking of and that which I already knew that I finally realized where I was. I'd found my way back home at last.

The journey home takes us deep inside. But just as I've stressed the oneness of body and mind, I want to also stress the oneness of outside and inside. We need what is outside in order to reach what is inside. We need those still wild places in order to find the stillness within. And that is precisely why we now stand at a crossroads. Those still wild places could only guide me back to wholeness because they reminded me of something that was still deep inside of me. Sadly, though, it's now possible in this modern age for someone to grow to maturity without ever experiencing any real connection with the natural world from which we arise. What will life be like when our relationship with nature amounts to little more than a pleasant stroll past the exhibits of the local zoo during the best of times and a mortal struggle against disease and natural disaster during the worst? We stand at a crossroads because we risk losing touch forever with the stillness that can redeem us. What will become of us if we lose touch forever with that which we already know?

# Acknowledgements

Thank you for opening your heart to this work and trusting that it will touch you in a positive way. Thank you as well to all who've ever read my work and blessed me with constructive feedback or encouragement on this creative journey. I'm especially grateful to Mrs. Brewer, my fourth grade English teacher, who first instilled in me the awareness that I'm a writer. Finally, I'm grateful to all that ever found a home out there in the Nursery. Your life continues to nurture me in ways that this volume barely expresses.

# About the Author

Mark Robert Frank is a poet, blogger, and novelist. A contemplative from an early age, his writings continue to be influenced by the spiritual nurturance received in the woods behind his childhood home. It would take him decades of lived experience and formal Zen practice to fully appreciate the true nature of those formative years.

Mark holds a BS in education and MA in counseling psychology. He's been writing about spirituality, psychology, and nature for over ten years—first for Crossing Nebraska, then for Heartland Contemplative. That Which We Already Know is Mark's first published book-length work. He's currently finishing his first novel.